THE KRASL ART CENTER

ex libris

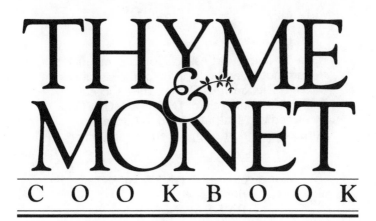

THYME & MONET

COOKBOOK

by

THE KRASL ART CENTER
St. Joseph, Michigan

THE COMMITTEE

Chairman:	Barbara Hall
Co-Chairman:	Mary Gates
Design Chairman:	Cay Beckmann
Marketing Chairman:	Vickie Florin
Recipe Coordinators:	Eugenie Cooper
	Mary Anne Wyse

PHOTOGRAPHY & STYLING
Palmini Schroeder & Salvino, Inc.

GRAPHIC DESIGN
Kris Hosbein, Sassafras Studio

The St. Joseph Art Association is committed to the promotion and education of the visual arts through The Krasl Art Center. The proceeds realized from the sale of **THYME & MONET** will be placed in a sculpture fund to further our purpose and to bring art to our community.

Additional copies of **THYME & MONET** may be obtained by writing:

THYME & MONET
Krasl Art Center
707 Lake Boulevard
St. Joseph, Michigan 49085
(616) 983-0271

Please enclose your return address with a check payable to **Krasl Art Center— THYME & MONET** in the amount of $16.95 per book plus $3.00 postage and handling. Michigan residents add sales tax.

For your convenience, order blanks are included in the back of the book.

Printed in the USA by
WIMMER BROTHERS
A Wimmer Company
Memphis • Dallas

What is as pleasing as a beautifully prepared plate of sumptuous food?... Michelangelo's "David", ... Renoir's "Luncheon of the Boating Party", ...: Andrew Wyeth's "Christina's World"? ... Food and art are two of life's most satisfying pleasures and both are equally gratifying. While art enriches our souls and magnifies our enjoyment of everyday living, food energizes our bodies and delights our eyes as well as our palates. By varying food textures, colors, and serving pieces, ordinary meals can be transformed into works of art. Cooking can be as imaginative as it is delicious. Meals are a celebration of food; art is a celebration of life.

Just as food is part of our lives, so is art. Here in St. Joseph, we are privileged to have one of Southwestern Michigan's leading art resources ... The Krasl Art Center. The Krasl is comfortably nestled in St. Joseph's historical district, directly across from Lake Bluff Park ... overlooking Lake Michigan.

Both The Krasl Art Center and St. Joseph have experienced a decade of energetic development. The buildings, unique shops, summer concerts, Venetian Festival, and Art Fair have all made St. Joseph a charming and desirable place in which to live and visit. The Krasl has firmly established itself as a significant addition to the City and stands as one of its cultural cornerstones.

In 1962 several local artists organized to sponsor an annual art fair. As the St. Joseph Art Fair grew in status and popularity, the group known as the St. Joseph Art Association developed a second objective: to establish a community art center.

The Association's dream was realized in 1976 when George J. Krasl, a St. Joseph industrialist, left a trust to build and maintain this longed-for facility. In July of 1980, the Association moved into the impressive new Krasl Art Center. Residents and visitors alike appreciate The Center's many educational offerings: exhibitions, classes, lectures, music programs, and trips.

THYME & MONET is a collection of favorite recipes received from The Krasl's members and friends. It features simple contemporary dishes and elegant gourmet feasts. We have enhanced **THYME & MONET** with beautiful color photographs, which truly blend food and art as one.

We hope you enjoy this cookbook. The proceeds will be placed into the Krasl Sculpture Fund. **THYME & MONET** is dedicated to The Krasl on its tenth anniversary ... to Olga Krasl, its benefactress, on her ninetieth birthday ... and to the art of beautiful food.

THANK YOU

A special thank you to the following artists and merchants who contributed their works and services for the photography.

Contributing Artists:
Lois Wolf Reilly
Betts Rittmeyer
Bill Cooper
Becky Rotter
Steve Hess
Tod Villeneuve
Kathy Sheldon
Charles Hires Sr.
Jerry Catania
Kathy Bundy
Dave Nelson

Contributing Merchants
Marty Bass, B.H. Fruit Market
James Lee
The Mole Hole
Meskimens

Additional Thanks:
Vicky Nemethy
Bonnie Merrifield

We lovingly dedicate this book to Olga Krasl.

Choc mousse cake
Pumpkin Torte

The Committee wishes to thank these friends who contributed so generously to this project: Krasl Board of Directors, Dar Davis, Executive Director and the Krasl Staff. We offer a special thanks to our families for their support.

This book would not have been possible without the unselfish sharing of treasured recipes by Krasl members and friends. The testing of these recipes has been a joy. We have made every effort to make this book free from errors for your enjoyment. Bon appétit!

TABLE OF CONTENTS

Cover photo:
TWO GARDENS SALAD
recipe on page 81

MICHIGAN BOUNTY
CORNISH HENS
Recipe on page 173

CLASSIC CHEESE & ASPIC
APPETIZERS
Recipe on page 29

SPAGHETTI WITH
SHIITAKE & TOMATO CREAM SAUCE
Recipe on page 142

CREAM OF CARROT SOUP
Recipe on page 56

SESAME CRACKERS, POP OVERS
& CRUSTY COUNTRY BREAD
Recipes on pages 115, 109 & 122

CROWN ROAST OF PORK
Recipe on page 209

WATERMELON SLICE SORBET
Recipe on page 267

EDIBLE WATER LILIES
Recipe on page 243

APPETIZERS

SHOE PEG CORN SPREAD

1	12-ounce can white shoe peg corn, drained
4	ounces Cheddar cheese, shredded
½	cup Parmesan cheese, grated
1	cup sour cream
½	cup mayonnaise
1	tablespoon grated onion

Mix all ingredients together and chill. Flavor improves if allowed to rest overnight in the refrigerator. Serve with crackers.

LAYERED SHRIMP SPREAD

8	ounces cream cheese, softened
1	hard cooked egg, chopped fine
3	tablespoons mayonnaise
½	teaspoon curry powder
1	4-ounce can baby shrimp, drained
4	green onions, finely chopped

Mix cream cheese, egg, mayonnaise and curry powder. Spread in an 8" pie plate. Cover with shrimp and onions. Serve with crackers.
12 appetizer servings.

SHRIMP DIP

½	pound small shrimp, cooked
3	ounces cream cheese, softened
1	small onion, grated
¼	cup mayonnaise
⅛	cup ketchup
½	teaspoon prepared horseradish
Dash of hot pepper sauce	

Mix all of the ingredients well and chill. Serve with crackers.

CURRY DIP

2	cups chicken broth
1	tablespoon curry powder
2	envelopes unflavored gelatin
1½	cups mayonnaise

Soften gelatin in ½ cup cool broth. Heat remaining 1½ cups of broth and blend well with mayonnaise and curry powder. Add gelatin mixture and strain into an oiled mold. Chill until firm. Unmold and serve with crackers.

RAW RADISH DIP

1	cup radishes, finely chopped
1	8 ounce package cream cheese, room temperature
1	clove garlic, minced
1	tablespoon fresh lemon juice
¾	teaspoon salt
½	teaspoon dried dillweed
Dash of freshly ground pepper	
Parsley sprigs and radish slices (garnish)	
Assorted crudités	

Combine first 6 ingredients and mix well. Season with pepper. Turn into serving dish, cover and chill 4 hours. Garnish with parsley and radish slices and serve with crudités.
8 to 10 servings.

CHEESE-ONION SOUFFLÉ

2	cups mayonnaise
1	cup ripe olives, sliced
2	cups thinly sliced onions
1	cup Cheddar cheese, shredded
1	cup Swiss cheese, shredded

Combine ingredients in order listed; pour into a 2 quart casserole. Bake in a 350 degree oven for 30 minutes. Serve warm with party rye bread or crackers.
12-16 appetizer servings.

CANDY'S HOT ARTICHOKE DIP

**1 14-ounce can artichokes (do
not use marinated)**

½ cup Parmesan cheese, grated

¾ cup mayonnaise

**1 4-ounce can chopped mild
green chilies, drained**

Drain and chop artichokes. Add
remaining ingredients; pour into a
small pie plate. Bake in a 350
degree oven until hot and bubbly,
30 minutes. Serve with tortilla chips
or crackers.
12-14 appetizer servings.

HOT CURRIED CLAM DIP

**8 ounces cream cheese with
chives**

1 7½-ounce can minced clams

**2 tablespoons Worcestershire
sauce**

¾ teaspoon curry powder

Dash of red pepper sauce

Drain clams; reserve liquid to use if
more moisture is needed. Warm
cheese in a small skillet. Add clams,
Worcestershire sauce, curry powder
and pepper sauce. Mix well; heat
until mixture is hot, but not boiling,
stirring occasionally. Serve in a
warm dish with crackers.

HOT CLAM DIP

2	5-ounce jars sharp cheese
½	bunch green onions and stems, chopped
¼	green pepper, finely chopped
2	dashes paprika
2	dashes hot pepper sauce
½	teaspoon garlic salt
1	tablespoon Worcestershire sauce
1	can minced clams, drained, 1 tablespoon liquid reserved
1	small jar chopped pimento, drained

Mix all ingredients and heat. Serve in a chafing dish with tortilla chips.

BLACK BEAN DIP

1	pound ground beef
1	onion, grated
1	can black beans or black bean soup
¾	cup ketchup
1	tablespoon Worcestershire sauce
½	teaspoon garlic powder
1	teaspoon oregano
1	tablespoon chili powder
3-4 drops hot pepper sauce	

Brown ground beef and onion; drain fat. Purée black beans in a blender (this is not necessary if bean soup is used). Add beans to beef along with the ketchup and seasonings. Cook 5 minutes, stirring often. Serve warm with corn chips for dipping.

HOT POTATO DIP

8	ounces cream cheese, softened
1	can cream of potato soup
1	teaspoon prepared horseradish
1	tablespoon dried onion flakes
¼	teaspoon pepper
1	4½-ounce can tiny shrimp, rinsed and drained
⅓	cup chopped almonds
8	ounces Cheddar cheese, shredded

Mix cream cheese, soup, horseradish, onion and pepper with an electric mixer. Spread half of this mixture in a shallow 8" x 8" baking dish. Sprinkle shrimp and almonds on top, then half of the Cheddar. Top with the remaining potato mixture and the rest of the Cheddar. Bake in a 350 degree oven for 20-25 minutes. Cool 10-15 minutes before serving with crackers.
10 appetizer servings.

CHICKEN LIVER PÂTÉ

6	slices bacon
½	pound chicken livers
1	small onion, quartered
1	tablespoon mustard
1	teaspoon vinegar
½	cup sour cream

Sauté bacon until it is limp. Remove from skillet; add chicken livers to bacon drippings and sauté until no longer pink inside. Put all ingredients into a blender or food processor and process until smooth. Flavor improves if made ahead and chilled several hours.
8-10 appetizer servings.

WILHELMINA'S LIVER PÂTÉ

1-2 tablespoons margarine

1   small onion, chopped

½-¾ pound chicken livers

2   hard cooked eggs, chopped

¼   teaspoon garlic juice

Salt and pepper to taste

Brown onion in margarine and add chicken livers; simmer until livers are slightly pink inside. Chop livers in pan with a spoon; add eggs, garlic juice, salt and pepper. Add margarine as needed for spreading consistency.
8-10 appetizer servings.

HERRING APPETIZERS

1   pint herring tidbits in wine sauce

1   cup sour cream

½   cup mayonnaise

1   teaspoon sugar

1   teaspoon lemon juice

1   teaspoon celery seeds

1   bunch green onions, sliced

4   teaspoons green pepper, chopped

Drain herring and cut into bite sized pieces. Mix remaining ingredients and stir in herring. Chill several hours before serving with crackers.

PARMESAN STUFFED SHRIMP

1	cup round buttery cracker crumbs
½	cup margarine, melted
¼	cup Parmesan cheese, grated
1½	tablespoons dry vermouth
1	teaspoon lemon juice
½	teaspoon garlic salt or powder
16	jumbo shrimp, peeled and deveined

Combine all ingredients except shrimp; set aside. Butterfly shrimp and fill with cracker mixture. Arrange shrimp in a baking dish and bake in a 250 degree oven for 25 minutes. Place under the broiler for 1 minute or until lightly browned.
4 servings.

SHRIMP CITRUS

3	pounds shrimp, shelled and deveined
5	oranges, peeled and sectioned
5	medium white onions, sliced
1½	cups cider vinegar
1	cup vegetable oil
⅔	cup fresh lemon juice
½	cup ketchup
¼	cup sugar
3	tablespoons capers, drained
3	tablespoons parsley, minced
2	teaspoons salt
2	teaspoons mustard seeds
1	teaspoon celery seeds
¼	teaspoon pepper
3	cloves garlic, crushed
1	lemon, thinly sliced for garnish

Cook shrimp in boiling water for 2 minutes. Rinse immediately in cold water until thoroughly cool; drain. Put shrimp, oranges, and onion in a large bowl. Mix remaining ingredients, except lemon; pour over shrimp. Cover and refrigerate 8 hours or overnight, stirring occasionally. Serve on a bed of lettuce garnished with lemon slices. Note: Shrimp should be slightly undercooked as it will continue to become firm in the marinade.
12-15 appetizer servings.

APPETIZERS

INDIAN CURRY CHEESE BALL

3	8-ounce packages cream cheese, softened
¾	teaspoon dry mustard
3	tablespoons curry powder
¾	cup peach chutney
¾	cup slivered almonds, toasted
3	ounces shredded coconut

Combine cream cheese, dry mustard and curry powder. Mix well. Add chutney and slivered almonds. Shape into a ball and roll in coconut.

GOUDA POUPON

8	ounce round gouda cheese
1	can crescent dinner rolls
Dijon mustard	

Have cheese at room temperature. Remove wax covering from the cheese. Unwrap the crescent rolls sealing together to form 2 squares, one for the bottom and the other for the top of cheese; work the dough around the cheese. Be sure to wrap securely to keep the cheese from leaking out. Bake on a cookie sheet at 375 degrees approximately 20-30 minutes or until completely browned. Put on a cheese board to serve. Make small pie wedge slices and spread with Dijon mustard.

APPETIZER APPLE SLICES

3-4 red apples	
3	**ounces cream cheese, softened**
2	**tablespoons chopped dates**
2	**tablespoons chopped almonds**
1	**tablespoon sherry**
Lemon juice	

Thinly slice apples; put into a plastic bag with a small amount of lemon juice to keep them from discoloring. Mix cream cheese, dates, almonds and sherry and mound on apple slices. Slices will keep several hours, covered, in the refrigerator.
Yield: 24 slices.

BLEU CHEESE NIBBLES

1	**8-ounce package refrigerated biscuits**
½	**cup butter**
8	**tablespoons bleu cheese, crumbled**

Quarter each biscuit; arrange in 2 round cake pans. Melt butter and bleu cheese together and pour over biscuits. Bake in a 400 degree oven for 12-15 minutes. Serve warm.
Yield: 40 nibbles.

MAGIC MUSHROOMS

2	**pounds spicy Italian sausage**
2	**pounds fresh mushrooms**

Clean mushrooms. Remove stems and chop. Mix chopped stems with the sausage. Form into walnut size balls and place in mushroom cap so that the mix extends over the top of the mushroom. Place the stuffed mushrooms in a 9" x 13" baking dish. Bake in a 350 degree oven for 30 minutes or until browned.
Yield: 40 mushrooms.

APPETIZERS

DEVILED MUSHROOMS

1   small onion, minced
2   tablespoons butter
3   slices white bread, toasted and cut into ½″ cubes
½   teaspoon salt
¼   teaspoon pepper
½   teaspoon garlic powder
½   cup beef broth, milk or water
2   teaspoons soy sauce
12-16 large mushroom caps

Sauté onion in butter for 5 minutes. Add bread, seasonings, broth and soy sauce. Mound mixture into mushroom caps. Place mushrooms in a buttered baking dish. Bake in a 350 degree oven for 15 minutes.

RIDGEWAY BRIDGE SANDWICHES

6   ounces Swiss cheese, shredded
1   small red onion, finely chopped
Mayonnaise
White bread, quartered, crusts cut off

Mix Swiss cheese and onion with enough mayonnaise to make everything stick together. Spread on bread, cover and refrigerate several hours before serving. Yield: 1½ cups of spread.

TINY CHICKEN QUICHES

Dough for two 9" pie crusts

1 4½-ounce can of chicken spread

3 wedges Gruyère cheese, shredded

2 eggs

¼ cup cream

Pepper to taste

Roll dough thin; cut into 24 2½" circles. Fit pastry into 1½" muffin tins. Add ½ teaspoon chicken spread and a small amount of shredded cheese to each. Beat eggs; stir in cream and pepper. Fill each cup with about 1½ teaspoons of egg mixture. Bake in a 400 degree oven for 18-20 minutes. Cool 1 minute before removing from pans.
Yield: 24 appetizer servings.

BABY BURGERS

½ **pound butter, melted**

1½ **tablespoons poppy seeds**

1½ **tablespoons dry mustard**

½ **tablespoon onion powder**

½ **tablespoon garlic powder**

1 **pound lean ground beef**

1 **egg, well beaten**

1 **6-8-ounce block sharp Cheddar cheese**

3 **20 count packages party rolls**

Mix butter, poppy seeds, dry mustard, onion powder and garlic powder; set aside. Stir egg into ground beef. Slice rolls in half; brush inside surfaces with butter mixture. Put a bit of beef and a tiny piece of cheese on the bottom of each roll. Put on tops and place burgers back in their foil pans. Cover with additional foil and bake in a 350 degree oven for 30 minutes.
Yield: 60 baby burgers.

SISSY CAKES

1	pound bacon, fried crisp and drained
2	stalks celery, chopped
1	small onion, chopped
6	mushrooms, chopped
1	teaspoon dry mustard
1	teaspoon seasoned salt
½	cup mozzarella cheese, shredded
1¼	cups Cheddar cheese, shredded
3	tablespoons prepared mustard
Mayonnaise	
1	loaf cocktail rye bread

Crumble bacon in a bowl; add celery, onion, mushrooms, dry mustard, seasoned salt and cheeses. Mix well. Add prepared mustard and enough mayonnaise to hold mixture together. Top each slice of bread with 1 tablespoon of the mixture. Bake on a large cookie sheet in a 350 degree oven for 10 minutes or until bubbly.
Yield: 3 dozen pieces.

MEXICAN FUDGE

8	ounces Cheddar cheese, shredded
8	ounces Monterey Jack cheese, shredded
½	cup salsa
3	eggs

Combine cheeses in a bowl. Beat together eggs and salsa in a small bowl. Place ½ of the cheese mixture in an 8" x 8" baking pan; pour salsa and egg mixture over the cheese. Top with remaining cheese. Bake in a 350 degree oven for 25 minutes. Cool slightly and cut into squares. Serve accompanied by tortilla chips.
Yield: 16 squares.

TORTILLA PINWHEELS

8	ounces sour cream
8	ounces cream cheese, softened
1	4-ounce can chopped green chilies
1	4-ounce can chopped black olives, drained
1	cup Cheddar cheese, shredded
½	cup green pepper, chopped
Garlic powder to taste	
Seasoned salt to taste	
½	cup salsa
5	10" flour tortillas
Fresh parsley for garnish	

Mix first nine ingredients thoroughly. Divide filling and spread over tortillas. Roll up tortillas and wrap each tightly in plastic wrap, twisting ends. Refrigerate for several hours. Before serving unwrap and cut rolls into ½" thick slices. Serve garnished with parsley.
Yield: 40 appetizers.

TACO PIZZA

2	packages refrigerated crescent shaped rolls
1	cup sour cream
1	8-ounce package cream cheese, room temperature
1	package taco seasoning
1	pound lean ground beef
Chopped onion	
Chopped tomato	
Shredded lettuce	
Shredded cheese	
Optional: black olives, green peppers, sliced mushrooms	

Pat rolls into an 11" x 15" pan, pinching edges together. Bake according to package directions. Cool. Brown ground beef; drain. Mix meat with ½ package of taco seasoning. Cool. Mix cream cheese, sour cream and the remaining taco seasoning. Spread onto cooled crust. Top with ground beef mixture. Top with onion, tomato, lettuce, cheese and optional toppings as desired. Cut into squares for serving.
Yield: 48 squares.

BLUE CORNMEAL CRACKERS

¾ cup plus 1 tablespoon blue cornmeal, divided

½ cup flour

¼ teaspoon salt

⅓ cup margarine, softened

¼ cup skim milk

Cayenne to taste

Seasoned salt to taste

Combine ¾ cup cornmeal, flour and salt in a small bowl. Cut in margarine. (This may also be done in a food processor with a few short pulses.) Sprinkle milk over mixture and stir until moist. Turn onto a floured board and knead 5 or 6 times. Flatten dough slightly, wrap in plastic and chill 20-30 minutes.

On a floured board roll dough out to ⅛″ thickness and cut into 2″ rounds. Place on ungreased baking sheets and sprinkle with cornmeal which has been seasoned with cayenne and seasoned salt. Bake in a preheated 350 degree oven for 8-10 minutes. Yield: 3½ dozen crackers.

HARVEST POPCORN

⅓ cup butter

1 teaspoon dried dillweed

1 teaspoon lemon pepper

1 teaspoon Worcestershire sauce

½ teaspoon garlic powder

½ teaspoon onion powder

¼ teaspoon salt

2 cups canned shoestring potatoes

1 cup mixed nuts

2 quarts popped corn (⅓ cup unpopped kernels)

In a small saucepan melt butter. Add seasonings and mix well. Stir in shoestring potatoes and nuts. Pour over popcorn and toss well. Spread on a jelly roll pan and bake in a 350 degree oven for 6-8 minutes. Stir once during baking. Cool and store in an airtight container.

SPICED COCKTAIL NUTS

1	pound large pecan halves
1	egg white, room temperature
2	tablespoons cold water
½	cup sugar
½	teaspoon cinnamon
¼	teaspoon allspice
¼	teaspoon chili powder

Beat egg white and water until frothy. Add pecans and mix until coated. Combine sugar, cinnamon, allspice and chili powder. Pour over pecans and mix well. Spread pecans on a buttered cookie sheet. Bake in a 225 degree oven 1½-2 hours, stirring occasionally. (Pecans should look dry.) Cool and store in a tightly covered container.

VANILLA WALNUTS

1	pound walnut halves
½	cup sugar
2½	tablespoons corn oil
1	4" long vanilla bean, pulverized or finely minced to a paste*
¼	teaspoon salt
¼	teaspoon pepper
¼	teaspoon ground coriander
¼	teaspoon cinnamon
¼	teaspoon nutmeg
¼	teaspoon allspice

Preheat oven to 325 degrees. Blanch walnuts for 1 minute in boiling water; drain well. While walnuts are still hot, put them in a bowl and toss with the sugar and corn oil. Let stand 10 minutes. Arrange on a rimmed baking tray. Bake for 30-35 minutes, turning every 5-10 minutes until nuts are light brown and crispy. Combine the vanilla and seasonings and toss with the hot nuts. Spread in a single layer to cool. Store airtight.
*Instead of the vanilla bean, you may substitute 1 tablespoon of vanilla extract. Blend it with the corn oil before tossing with the nuts.

BACON STUFFED AVOCADOS

4   ripe avocados
Lemon juice
1½ pounds thick sliced bacon
¼   cup cider vinegar
¼   cup sugar
¼   cup ketchup
¼   cup water
Salt and pepper to taste

Cut avocados in half and peel. Remove seeds and brush with lemon juice to prevent discoloration. Set aside. Cut bacon into small pieces and cook until not quite crisp. Remove bacon pieces from pan and drain on paper towels; set aside. Pour off all but 3-4 tablespoons of the bacon grease. Add to the pan the vinegar, sugar, ketchup and water. Heat to boiling. Add bacon to pan. Remove from heat and add salt and pepper. Divide bacon mixture among the avocado halves.
8 first course servings.

ALMOND BRANDY MOLD

12 ounces cream cheese, softened
½   cup butter, room temperature
½   cup sour cream
½   cup sugar
1   envelope gelatin
¼   cup cold water
1   cup slivered almonds
Grated rind of 2 lemons
1   cup white raisins, soaked overnight in brandy to cover

Beat together cream cheese, butter, sour cream and sugar. Dissolve gelatin in cold water in a double boiler over hot water. Combine with cheese mixture. Add almonds, lemon rind and presoaked, drained raisins. Pour into a very well oiled mold. Chill until firm. Unmold and serve with crackers or apple slices.

CHARLESTON CRAB MOUSSE

½	can condensed tomato soup
4	ounces cream cheese
1	tablespoon unflavored gelatin
⅛	cup cold water
½	cup mayonnaise
½	cup chopped celery
½	large onion, chopped
½	pound crabmeat
½	teaspoon Worcestershire sauce
1	tablespoon horseradish

Salt and pepper to taste

Dash of hot pepper sauce

Olives and slivered almonds for garnish

Heat soup and add cream cheese; stir until melted. Soften gelatin in cold water and add to the hot soup. Cool. Add mayonnaise, celery, onion, crabmeat and seasonings. Turn into a buttered fish mold and chill overnight. Unmold and decorate with olives for eyes and almonds for scales. Serve with light crackers.

CLASSIC CHEESE AND ASPIC

½	envelope unflavored gelatin (½ tablespoon)
3	tablespoons cold water
¾	cup cold beef stock or bouillon
2	tablespoons white or blush wine
1	tablespoon fresh lemon juice, strained
4	dashes hot pepper sauce
1½	pounds sharp Cheddar cheese, sliced ⅛″ - ¼″ thick
Pumpernickel bread, cocktail size	
For garnish: mild herbs, pimento, green onions, cheese	

In a quart bowl sprinkle gelatin over cold water to soften. Bring ¼ cup of stock to a boil and pour over softened gelatin, stirring until dissolved. Stir in remaining cold stock, wine, lemon juice and hot pepper sauce. Refrigerate until aspic mixture has the consistency of warm egg whites.

In the meantime cut the cheese into various decorative shapes, slightly smaller than the bread slices. Place cheese on cookie sheets and cover with plastic wrap until ready to use. When aspic has reached desired consistency, spoon or brush over each cheese shape to form a thin layer. Refrigerate, covered, until aspic is firm. Remove from refrigerator and press garnishes into aspic. Coat with another layer of aspic; cover and refrigerate until firm. To serve, place each cheese shape on a slice of cocktail bread and arrange on a platter.
Yield: 40 appetizers.

See photo illustration.

PINK PEPPERCORN PÂTÉ

8 whole skinless, boneless chicken breasts, cut into ½″ pieces

1 cup plus 3 tablespoons snipped chives

5 tablespoons fresh tarragon, chopped

1¼ cups finely diced ham

½ cup shelled pistachios

5 tablespoons pink peppercorns

⅔ cup brandy

2 teaspoons salt

1 teaspoon ground pepper

2 large eggs

2 large egg whites

½ teaspoon grated nutmeg

2½ cups whipping cream

Place ¼ of the chicken in a large bowl. Add 1 cup chives, 3 tablespoons tarragon, ham, pistachios, pink peppercorns, ⅓ cup brandy, salt and pepper; toss together. Let mixture marinate at room temperature for 30 minutes.

Place remaining chicken in a food processor fitted with a metal blade and process until meat is ground. Add eggs and egg whites and process until smooth. Add the remaining ⅓ cup brandy, 3 tablespoons chives, 2 tablespoons tarragon and nutmeg; process until blended. With the motor running, add the whipping cream through the feed tube; process until smooth.

Add the processed mixture to the marinated mixture and stir until combined. Turn into an oiled 16″ x 5″ loaf pan. Cover with foil.

Place pan in a shallow baking pan. Add enough hot water to come halfway up the sides of the loaf pan. Bake in a preheated 350 degree oven for 1 hour or until top of pâté is firm to the touch. Let cool at room temperature. Invert and wrap in plastic wrap. Refrigerate until ready to serve.

APPLE WALNUT PÂTÉ

1	cup walnuts
1	medium onion, quartered
2	shallots, peeled
1	large tart apple, peeled, seeded and quartered
6	tablespoons butter, divided
2	tablespoons vegetable oil, divided
8	ounces hot, spicy pork sausage
1	pound chicken livers
2	teaspoons Cognac or brandy
2	teaspoons dried tarragon
⅛	teaspoon allspice
⅛	teaspoon dried thyme
1	teaspoon garlic powder
2	teaspoons salt
½	teaspoon white pepper
8	ounces cream cheese, softened and cubed

In a food processor fitted with a metal blade, chop walnuts for 5 seconds. Remove and set aside. Using same bowl mince onion, shallots and apple. Melt 3 tablespoons butter and 1 tablespoon oil in a large frying pan and sauté onion, shallot and apple mixture until onion is transparent. Remove mixture from pan and set aside. To the same pan add the remaining 3 tablespoons butter and 1 tablespoon oil and sauté the sausage and chicken livers until done, at least 10 minutes. Drain fat. Heat brandy and pour over sausage and liver.

Combine liver and apple mixtures and return to food processor; process for 30 seconds. Add seasonings and cream cheese and process until smooth. Add walnuts and process briefly, 3 or 4 quick pulses. Spoon into a lightly oiled 3 cup mold and chill until firm. Unmold and serve with crackers.

WINTER SALSA

28 ounce can crushed tomatoes
with added pureé

1 or 2 4-ounce cans chopped
green chilies, drained

1 small onion, chopped

1 or 2 tomatoes (no matter how
lousy), roughly chopped

1 green pepper, chopped

Liquid from bottled jalapeño
peppers, to taste

Combine all ingredients in glass
bowl. Let stand 30 minutes to
blend. Add more liquid from
jalapeño if too mild. Cook's note:
Add more fresh tomato and green
pepper if you want chunkier salsa.

Optional — garlic, fresh cilantro, a
little rice vinegar, chopped green
onion.

MIXED FRUIT CHUTNEY

5 pounds tomatoes, peeled,
seeded and chopped

2 pounds peaches, peeled and
chopped

2 pounds pears, peeled and
chopped

3 onions, chopped

2 green peppers, chopped

1 or more dried red chili
peppers, crushed

2 tablespoons chopped fresh
ginger root or crystalized ginger

1½ tablespoons salt

3 cups sugar

3 cups cider vinegar

¼ cup mixed pickling spices, tied
in cheesecloth

In large enamel or stainless steel
pan combine all the ingredients
and bring to a boil, stirring
constantly. Reduce heat to low and
simmer, uncovered, for 2½ hours or
until thick, stirring frequently.
Remove spice bag, ladle into
sterilized jars. Will keep for about 2
weeks in refrigerator.
Makes about 5 pints. Serve over
cream cheese with crackers.

BRUNCH

KAFFI KRINGLA

CRUST:

1 cup flour

½ cup butter or margarine

1 tablespoon water

PUFF LAYER:

1 cup water

½ cup butter or margarine

¾ cup flour

3 eggs

½ teaspoon almond or
1 teaspoon vanilla extract

GLAZE:

1 cup confectioners sugar

½ teaspoon almond extract

2-3 tablespoons milk

To make the crust, work the flour and margarine together with the fingers. Add 1 tablespoon of water, if necessary to make dough stick together. Pat crust out onto a large baking sheet in 2 rows, each 3" wide.

To make the puff layer, bring 1 cup of water to a boil along with the butter. Beat in the flour until mixture forms a ball and pulls away from the sides of the pan. Remove from heat and beat in eggs, one at a time. Add almond or vanilla extract. Mixture should be very stiff. Spoon evenly onto the 2 crust layers. Bake in a preheated 350 degree oven for 50 minutes or until top is browned and dry. Cool completely.

Make glaze by mixing confectioners sugar with almond extract and just enough milk to blend. Spread glaze over cooled coffeecakes and top with chopped almonds, if desired.

BLUEBERRY CHEESE COFFEECAKE

2	cups flour
1	cup oat bran
4	teaspoons baking powder
1	teaspoon salt
1	cup sugar
3	eggs, lightly beaten
½	cup sour cream
½	cup butter, melted
⅔	cup milk
1	teaspoon grated lemon peel
1	8-ounce package cream cheese, cut into ½" cubes
1½	cups blueberries

TOPPING:

¼	cup flour
1	teaspoon cinnamon
⅓	cup brown sugar
¼	cup cold butter, cut into pieces
½	cup chopped nuts

In a bowl combine flour, oat bran, baking powder, salt and sugar; set aside. In a large bowl combine the eggs, sour cream, butter and milk. Fold in the dry ingredients, lemon peel, cream cheese and blueberries, stirring until just combined. Spoon mixture into a greased 9" x 13" baking pan. To make the topping, mix the flour, cinnamon and brown sugar in a small bowl. Using the fingers, cut in the butter until mixture crumbles. Stir in nuts. Sprinkle topping over cake and bake in a preheated 350 degree oven for 55-60 minutes. Cool 15 minutes before cutting.

FRENCH CRUMB CAKE

½ cup butter

1 cup sugar

1 egg

1 teaspoon vanilla

2 cups flour

3 teaspoons baking powder

¾ cup milk

CRUMB TOPPING:

1 tablespoon butter, softened

2 tablespoons sugar

4 tablespoons flour

1 teaspoon cinnamon

Cream butter and sugar until fluffy. Add egg and vanilla and mix well. Combine flour and baking powder and add alternately with milk. Spread batter in a well-greased 9" x 9" baking pan. Combine topping ingredients, mixing with a fork until crumbled. Sprinkle over batter. Bake in a preheated 375 degree oven for 35-40 minutes. 9 servings.

CHERRY SWIRL COFFEECAKE

1½ cups sugar

½ cup butter or margarine, room temperature

½ cup solid vegetable shortening, room temperature

1½ teaspoons baking powder

1 teaspoon vanilla

1 teaspoon almond extract

4 eggs

3 cups flour

1 21-ounce can cherry pie filling

GLAZE:

1 cup confectioners sugar

1-2 tablespoons warmed milk

Grease a 15" x 10" jelly roll pan or 2 9" x 9" square pans; set aside. Blend sugar, butter, shortening, baking powder, vanilla, almond extract, and eggs in a large bowl and beat at low speed until mixed. Beat 3 minutes at high speed. Do not overbeat. Stir in flour just until mixed. Spread ⅔ of the batter in the jelly roll pan, or ⅓ in each of the 2 9" pans. Spread pie filling evenly over batter. Spoon the remaining batter evenly over the filling. Bake in a preheated 350 degree oven for 30-35 minutes. Mix the glaze ingredients until smooth and drizzle over the cake while warm.

ORANGE COFFEECAKE

1	egg
½	cup milk
½	cup sugar
½	teaspoon salt
2	tablespoons grated orange rind
2	cups flour
½	cup vegetable oil
½	cup orange juice
3	teaspoons baking powder

NUT TOPPING:

2	tablespoons margarine, room temperature
½	cup firmly packed brown sugar
½	cup chopped nuts or coconut
1	teaspoon cinnamon
1	teaspoon nutmeg

Beat egg. Add milk, sugar, salt, orange rind, ½ cup flour, oil and orange juice. Sift together remaining flour and baking powder. Fold flour into batter, stirring until just combined. Pour into a greased 8" x 8" square pan. To make topping, cream margarine and sugar; add nuts, cinnamon and nutmeg. Sprinkle topping over batter and bake in a 375 degree oven for 20-30 minutes.

GLORIA'S BAKED FRITTATA

¾	cup chopped red and green peppers
1½	cups sliced mushrooms
1½	cups chopped zucchini
¾	cup chopped onion
1	large clove garlic, minced
3	tablespoons unsalted butter
6	eggs, beaten
¼	cup half and half
½	pound Italian sausage, cooked, drained and crumbled
1	pound cream cheese, diced
1½	cups Cheddar cheese, shredded
2	cups cubed Italian bread
1	teaspoon salt
¼	teaspoon pepper

Sauté peppers, mushrooms, zucchini, onion and garlic in butter until zucchini is crisp-tender. Drain off excess liquid and cool slightly. Beat eggs with half and half. Add sausage, cream cheese, Cheddar cheese, bread cubes, salt, pepper and sautéed vegetables. Mix well and pour into a greased 10" springform pan. Bake in a 350 degree oven for 1 hour or until set in the center. Cool 10 minutes before cutting into wedges. 8 servings.

SEAFOOD QUICHE

1	9" pie shell, partially baked
½	pound mild white fish, or crabmeat, cooked and flaked
2	tablespoons onion, minced
2	tablespoons butter
1	3-ounce can mushrooms in broth, drained with broth reserved
4	eggs, beaten
¾	cup half and half
½	teaspoon salt
Dash cayenne	
⅛	teaspoon tarragon
¼	teaspoon marjoram
⅛	teaspoon pepper
½	cup Swiss cheese, shredded

Sauté onion in butter. Set aside several mushrooms, putting the remainder in the pan with the onions. Sauté until softened. Combine eggs, half and half, mushroom broth and seasonings. Fold in onions, mushrooms and flaked fish. Pour into prepared pie shell. Sprinkle with cheese and bake in a 375 degree oven for 20 minutes. Top with the reserved mushrooms and continue to bake for 15 minutes or until set. Let stand 5 minutes before cutting. Garnish with paprika.
6 servings.

DENVER PITAS

½	cup chopped onion
½	cup chopped green pepper
2	tablespoons butter or margarine
6	eggs
8	slices bacon, cooked and crumbled
Salt and pepper to taste	
3	large pita breads

In a large skillet sauté onion and pepper in butter until tender. Beat eggs slightly; stir in bacon, salt and pepper. Pour egg mixture into skillet and cook over low heat, gently lifting cooked portions and tilting pan to allow uncooked portion to flow to the bottom of the pan. Cook until eggs are firm, but still moist, 3-5 minutes. Cut the pitas in half and fill with egg mixture.
6 servings.

OMELETTE #14

8	slices white bread, buttered
1	pound Monterey Jack cheese, shredded
1	pound lean sausage, cooked, drained and crumbled, optional
3	4-ounce cans chopped green chilies, drained
10	large eggs
3	cups milk
¾	teaspoon salt, or to taste
¾	teaspoon dry mustard
Dash of cayenne	

Cut bread into 1" cubes and place in a greased 9" x 13" pan. Sprinkle cheese over bread. Spread on sausage, if used, followed by chilies. Beat eggs, milk and seasonings together and pour over layered ingredients. Cover and refrigerate overnight. Bake, covered, in a 350 degree oven for 1 hour. Uncover and continue to bake for 5 minutes, or until browned. Serve with MELON SALSA.
8-10 servings.

MELON SALSA

1	medium honeydew melon, peeled, seeded and diced
1	medium cantaloupe melon, peeled, seeded and diced
¼	cup fresh lime juice
¼	cup chopped fresh mint, or to taste
2	tablespoons olive oil
2	fresh jalapeño peppers, seeded and minced
Salt and pepper to taste	

Mix all of the ingredients in a glass bowl. Refrigerate at least 1 hour, or up to 24 hours. Served with grilled fish or OMELETTE #14.

AVOCADO CORN SALSA

¼	cup fresh or frozen corn kernels
1	medium avocado, peeled, seeded and chopped
1	medium tomato, peeled, seeded and chopped
½	small onion, minced
2	teaspoons cilantro, minced
2	teaspoons fresh lime juice
¼ - ½ jalapeño pepper, seeded and minced	

Simmer corn in 1 cup of water until tender; drain. Combine corn with remaining ingredients in a glass bowl. Cover and refrigerate up to 4 hours. Serve with grilled chicken or fish or as an omelette topping.

SOUR CREAM CHICKEN PIE

⅔	cup mayonnaise-style salad dressing
1	cup sour cream
1½	cups cooked chicken, cubed
1	9-ounce can pineapple tidbits, drained
1	cup chopped walnuts
½	cup celery, diced
2-3 tablespoons Parmesan cheese	
1	9" pastry shell, baked

Combine sour cream and salad dressing. Add ⅔ of the mixture to the chicken, along with the pineapple, walnuts and celery. Blend well and pour into the pie crust. Spread the remaining sour cream mixture carefully on top. Sprinkle with Parmesan and chill before serving.
6 servings.

GOLDEN DELIGHT PANCAKES

1	**cup creamed cottage cheese**
6	**eggs**
½	**cup flour**
¼	**teaspoon salt**
¼	**cup oil**
¼	**cup milk**
½	**teaspoon vanilla**

Put all of the ingredients in a blender. Cover and blend at high speed for 1 minute, stopping once to scrape down. Cook silver dollar size on a greased griddle.

MACADAMIA FRENCH TOAST

4	**eggs**
⅔	**cup orange juice**
⅓	**cup milk**
¼	**cup sugar, optional; omit if juice is sweet**
¼	**teaspoon ground nutmeg**
½	**teaspoon vanilla extract**
½	**loaf of Italian or French bread, cut into 1" slices**
⅓	**cup butter**
½	**cup macadamia nuts, coarsely chopped**

Beat eggs, orange juice, milk, sugar, nutmeg and vanilla, using a whisk or mixer. Place bread in a single layer in a 15" x 10" baking pan so that bread fits tightly. Pour the egg mixture over bread and refrigerate overnight, turning once.

Preheat oven to 400 degrees. Melt butter on a non-stick jelly roll pan in the oven. Arrange bread slices on the pan and sprinkle with the macadamia nuts. Bake 20-25 minutes, or until golden brown. Serve with butter, maple syrup or a sprinkling of confectioners sugar. 4 servings.

HAM AND GREEN BEAN CASSEROLE

2	10-ounce packages frozen whole green beans
1	pound sliced fresh mushrooms, 3 reserved for garnish
¼	cup butter
⅓	cup flour
2	cups milk
1	5¾-ounce can evaporated milk
½	teaspoon salt
⅛	teaspoon pepper
3	cups ham, cut into strips
⅓	cup pimento strips
Grated cheese for garnish	

Cook green beans according to package directions; drain. Sauté the mushrooms in butter for 5 minutes. Stir in the flour and cook briefly. Add the milk, evaporated milk, salt and pepper and stir until thickened. Combine sauce with the beans, ham and pimento and pour into a 2 quart casserole. Top with grated cheese and reserved mushrooms. Bake in a 350 degree oven for 20 minutes, or until hot. 8 servings.

HOT CURRIED EGGS

12	hard cooked eggs, halved
1	tablespoon prepared mustard
1	teaspoon sugar
½	teaspoon salt
1	tablespoon melted butter
½	cup mayonnaise
1	tablespoon vinegar

CURRY SAUCE:

6	tablespoons margarine
6	tablespoons flour
1	teaspoon salt, or to taste
2	cups milk
1	teaspoon curry powder
¼	cup white wine
2-3	tablespoons capers, optional

Remove egg yolks from halved eggs, mash and mix with mustard, sugar, salt, butter, mayonnaise and vinegar. Spoon or pipe filling into egg whites and place in a shallow baking dish or casserole. For the sauce, combine all of the ingredients in a saucepan and cook over low heat for 10 minutes. Pour sauce over eggs and serve at once.

GREEN CHILI AND CHEESE PIE

1	9" unbaked pastry shell
1½	cups Monterey Jack cheese, shredded
1	cup Cheddar cheese, shredded
1	4-ounce can chopped green chilies, drained
1	cup half and half
3	eggs, lightly beaten
¼	teaspoon salt
⅛	teaspoon cumin

Preheat oven to 325 degrees. Partially bake pastry shell, 10 minutes; cool. Sprinkle all of the Monterey Jack cheese and half of the Cheddar over the bottom of the shell. Sprinkle chilies over the cheese. Beat half and half with eggs, salt and cumin until well blended. Pour egg mixture into the shell and sprinkle with the remaining Cheddar. Bake for 45 minutes, or until center of the pie is set. Let stand 15 minutes before serving. 6 servings.

BRUNCH

SHERRIED CHICKEN LIVERS

1	pound chicken livers
2	tablespoons sherry
2	tablespoons soy sauce
2	tablespoons cornstarch
1	teaspoon water
1	teaspoon sugar
2	tablespoons vegetable oil
¼-½ cup water	
3	bunches scallions, chopped to ¼″ thickness (include some green tops)
Grated fresh pepper to taste	

Rinse the chicken livers in fresh cold water; pat dry. Mix together the sherry, soy sauce, cornstarch, teaspoon of water and sugar. Blend well. Add the chicken livers and let stand 20 minutes. Heat 2 tablespoons of vegetable oil in a wok. Add the chicken livers and sauté for 3 minutes. Reduce heat and add ¼-½ cup water to wok. Add the chopped scallions; stir to blend. Let stand 5 minutes. Serve with rice. 2-4 servings.

SCOTTSBLUFF EGGS

12	eggs, beaten
2	17-ounce cans cream-style corn
2	4-ounce cans chopped green chilies, drained
2	cups sharp Cheddar cheese, shredded
2	cups Monterey Jack cheese, shredded
1	tablespoon instant grits
1½	teaspoons Worcestershire sauce
Dash pepper	

In a large bowl combine all the ingredients and beat until well blended. Pour into a greased 9″ x 13″ baking dish. Cover and refrigerate up to 24 hours. Remove from refrigerator 1 hour before baking. Bake in 325 degree oven for 1 hour, or until firm and lightly browned. 16 servings.

PATTI'S WONDERFUL PIE

4	tablespoons butter, divided
1½	pounds zucchini, sliced diagonally
½	pound large mushrooms, sliced
1	small, sweet onion, sliced
2	medium tomatoes, sliced
1	10" deep dish pastry shell, uncooked
1	cup mayonnaise
2	cups mozzarella cheese, shredded

Melt 3 tablespoons butter in a skillet and sauté zucchini until softened; remove from pan with a slotted spoon and drain on paper towel. Repeat with the mushrooms and onions. To assemble pie, spread remaining 1 tablespoon of softened butter over the pie shell. Place a layer of tomatoes in the bottom, followed by layers of zucchini, mushrooms and onion. Mix the mayonnaise with the shredded mozzarella and spread the mixture over the vegetables. Bake in a 350 degree oven for 1 hour. 6 servings.

CHEESE PUFF

1	cup butter
½	cup sugar
4	eggs
1½	cups milk
2	teaspoons baking powder
1½	cups flour
Pinch of salt	

FILLING:

2	pounds ricotta cheese
4	tablespoons butter, melted
2	eggs
2	tablespoons sugar
Pinch of salt	

Cream butter and sugar. Add eggs, one at a time. Blend in milk. Mix baking powder, flour and salt together and add to egg mixture. Mix all of the filling ingredients together; set aside. Spread ½ of the batter in a greased 9" x 13" baking pan. Carefully spread the filling over the batter and top with remaining batter. Cover and refrigerate overnight. Bake in a 350 degree oven for 45 minutes or until golden. Cut into squares and serve with sour cream and jelly or jam.

BRUNCH

GRITS SOUFFLÉ

1	quart milk
1	cup quick cooking grits
½	cup butter, room temperature
1½	teaspoons salt
⅛	teaspoon cayenne
3	cups shredded cheese such as Monterey Jack, jalapeño, or Jarlsberg
6	eggs, well beaten

Preheat oven to 350 degrees. In a saucepan heat the milk to the boiling point and whisk in the grits. Reduce heat and stir until mixture becomes the consistency of mush, 3-4 minutes. Remove from heat and add butter in pieces. Add the salt, cayenne and cheese, beating with a wooden spoon. (Dish may be prepared ahead to this point.) Before baking, beat in eggs and pour into a buttered 2½ quart casserole or soufflé dish. Bake uncovered for 1 hour and 10 minutes, or until puffed and golden. Recipe can easily be halved. Use a 1½ quart casserole and bake for 45-50 minutes. Full recipe serves 8.

MORNING GLORY STRATA

16	slices white bread, buttered, crusts trimmed
8	ounces Cheddar cheese, sliced
6	eggs, well beaten
1	quart milk
1	teaspoon salt
¼	teaspoon pepper
4	strips bacon, cooked crisp and crumbled
	Currant or grape jelly, optional

Arrange 8 slices of bread, buttered side down, in a 9" x 13" glass baking dish. Cover with the cheese and the remaining bread, buttered side up. Combine eggs, milk, salt and pepper and pour over bread. Cover and refrigerate overnight. Place baking pan in a larger pan and pour in hot water to come half way up the sides. Bake in a 300 degree oven for 1 hour, or until puffed and brown. Sprinkle bacon on top and serve with jelly, if desired.
8 servings.

BAKED PAPAYA

4	papayas, halved and seeded
1½	cups cottage cheese
11	ounces cream cheese, cubed, room temperature
4	tablespoons mango chutney
1	teaspoon curry powder
½	cup pecan halves
¼	cup sugar
½	teaspoon cinnamon
¼	cup butter, melted

In a medium bowl mix together the cottage cheese, cream cheese, mango chutney, curry powder and pecans. Fill the papaya halves with the mixture. Combine the cinnamon and sugar together. Sprinkle over the top of filled papayas. Drizzle melted butter over all. Bake in a preheated 450 degree oven for 15 minutes.
Serves 8.

PINEAPPLE DRESSING

⅓	cup butter or margarine, room temperature
¾	cup sugar
4	eggs
1	20-ounce can crushed pineapple
5	slices bread

Cream together butter and sugar. Beat in eggs. Drain the pineapple and blend in. Break up bread and fold in. Turn into a well-greased 2 quart baking dish. Bake in a 350 degree oven for 1 hour, or until browned.
6-8 servings.

SINFULLY SENSATIONAL DIP

8	ounces cream cheese, softened
1	cup whipped non-dairy topping
¾	cup brown sugar
⅓	cup Kahlua
1	cup sour cream

Mix the softened cream cheese with the rest of the ingredients. Blend thoroughly. Let stand 1 hour to blend flavors. Wonderful with fresh fruit.

SPARKLING PUNCH

2	12-ounce cans frozen lemonade concentrate
4	12-ounce cans water
1	46-ounce can unsweetened pineapple juice
2	liters lemon-lime soda
1	liter club soda

Mix lemonade, water and pineapple juice together. Add lemon-lime and club soda just before serving. Float lime slices in punch, if desired. Vodka may be added for an alcoholic punch.

HOT TOMATO JUICE COCKTAIL

2	24-ounce cans cocktail vegetable juice
4	beef bouillon cubes
3	cups hot water
3	teaspoons oregano
1	teaspoon celery salt
1½	teaspoons lemon juice
1	teaspoon horseradish
1	teaspoon Worcestershire sauce
2	tablespoons butter

Bring hot water to a boil and add bouillon cubes. Combine with remaining ingredients and simmer for 3 hours, stirring occasionally. Serve warm.

HOT BUTTERED RUM

1	pound brown sugar
½	cup unsalted butter
Dash of salt	
½	teaspoon nutmeg
½	teaspoon cloves
½	teaspoon cinnamon
Light or dark rum	
Hot milk	

In a mixing bowl cream brown sugar, butter and salt until smooth and fluffy. Beat in nutmeg, cloves and cinnamon. For each serving, drop 1 heaping tablespoon of the batter into a heated mug, add 1½-ounces of rum, stir and fill with hot milk. Batter may be stored, tightly covered, in the refrigerator.

SOUPS

ZESTY TOMATO SOUP

2	10½-ounce cans beef consommé
12	ounces tomato juice
1	stalk celery, roughly chopped
1	teaspoon Worcestershire sauce
1	teaspoon grated lemon rind
½	teaspoon sugar
2	bay leaves
Freshly ground black pepper	
Lemon slices for garnish	

Combine all ingredients except lemon slices in a saucepan and bring to a boil. Reduce heat and simmer 2-3 minutes. Remove celery and bay leaves. Serve in bowls or mugs garnished with lemon slices. 4 servings.

SHAKER CHICKEN SOUP

1	3-4 pound chicken, cooked and boned
3	quarts homemade chicken stock, fat skimmed
¼	cup dry vermouth
¼	cup butter
1	cup milk
8	ounces wide noodles
Salt and freshly ground pepper to taste	
Chopped parsley for garnish	

Combine one cup of broth, vermouth and butter. Bring to a boil and cook until reduced to ½ cup. Stir in milk. In the meantime cook noodles in the remaining broth until tender. Add milk mixture and diced chicken. Season with salt and pepper. Serve garnished with chopped parsley. Makes 8 servings.

CREAM OF CARROT SOUP

2	pounds carrots, peeled and chopped
4	cups water
4	chicken bouillon cubes
1	medium potato, peeled and chopped
1	teaspoon marjoram
1	teaspoon basil
3	tablespoons butter
1	medium onion, chopped
1	clove garlic, minced
⅓	cup sliced almonds
1	cup skim milk
½	cup sour cream
2	tablespoons dry vermouth
Watercress for garnish	

In a 4 quart Dutch oven combine carrots, water, bouillon, potato, marjoram and basil. Bring to a boil. Reduce heat and simmer, covered, 15 minutes or until vegetables are soft. Remove from heat and cool slightly. In a small skillet melt butter over medium heat. Add onion, garlic and almonds (reserve a few almonds for garnish) and sauté until onion is transparent. Combine carrot and onion mixtures in a food processor fitted with a metal blade and purée until smooth. It may be necessary to do this in two or three batches. Return the mixture to the Dutch oven; whisk in milk, sour cream and vermouth. Place over medium low heat and bring to serving temperature; do not boil. Garnish with watercress and reserved almonds.
Makes 6-8 servings.

See photo illustration.

QUICK WILD RICE SOUP

3	tablespoons margarine
½	cup celery, chopped
½	medium onion, chopped
3	tablespoons flour
½	teaspoon rosemary
Salt and pepper to taste	
1	14-ounce can chicken broth
2	cups milk
1	cup cooked wild rice
1	cup cooked chicken, cubed

In a medium saucepan melt margarine and sauté celery and onion until tender-crisp. Stir in flour, rosemary, salt and pepper. Add chicken broth and milk. Cook, stirring, until thickened. Add wild rice and chicken. Simmer for 2 minutes.
4 servings.

ITALIAN SPLIT PEA SOUP

1	cup split peas
4	cups water
4	beef bouillon cubes or 4 teaspoons bouillon granules

Freshly ground black pepper to taste

2	tablespoons olive oil
¼-½	pound Italian sausage, sweet or hot
1	cup celery, chopped
1	large onion, chopped
1	clove garlic, minced
½	cup red pepper, finely chopped
¼	cup dry red wine (substitute water if desired)

Grated Parmesan cheese to garnish

Hot red pepper sauce (optional)

Combine peas, water, bouillon and black pepper in a large saucepan. Heat to boiling; reduce heat and simmer. Cover and cook, stirring occasionally, until peas are tender. Meanwhile, cook sausage in olive oil, breaking the meat into small pieces. Add celery, onion, garlic and red pepper and sauté until tender (5 minutes). Add sausage and vegetable mixture to the soup, along with the wine, and simmer 15 minutes to blend flavors. Adjust thickness by cooking uncovered to thicken, or add water to thin. To serve, garnish with grated Parmesan and pass the red pepper sauce. 4-6 servings.

CORN SAUSAGE CHOWDER

1	pound bulk pork sausage
1	medium onion, chopped
⅓	cup green pepper, chopped
3	cups milk
2	17-ounce cans cream-style corn
12	ounces frozen hash brown potatoes, slightly thawed
1	can cream of mushroom or cream of celery soup
½	teaspoon salt, or to taste
¼	teaspoon dried tarragon or thyme
Freshly ground black pepper to taste	
4-6 ounces Cheddar cheese, shredded	

Cook sausage, onion, and green pepper in a large pot until meat is no longer pink. Drain fat. Add milk, corn, potatoes, soup, salt, tarragon and pepper. Heat to boiling, stirring constantly. Reduce heat and simmer, covered, until potatoes are tender, about 20 minutes, stirring occasionally. Stir in cheese and heat until melted.
Makes 8-10 servings.

BRUNSWICK STEW

3-4 pounds pork loin

3-3½ pound fryer (or stewing hen)

3 16-ounce cans tomatoes, undrained

1 8-ounce can tomato sauce

1½ cups onion, chopped

1 green pepper, chopped

1 red pepper, chopped

½ cup cider vinegar

¼ cup sugar

¼ cup flour

1 cup water

1 teaspoon salt, or to taste

Freshly ground black pepper to taste

1 teaspoon turmeric

4 teaspoons hot pepper sauce

1 tablespoon Worcestershire sauce

1 10-ounce package frozen corn

Roast pork until fully cooked (160 degrees on meat thermometer). Cool. Remove fat and cut meat into 2" - 3" pieces. Place chicken in a large pot, cover with water and simmer until tender, 1½ hours. Remove chicken from broth (reserve broth for another use). Discard skin and cut chicken into 2" - 3" pieces. Put pork and chicken in a food processor fitted with a metal blade. Chop coarsely. In a soup pot or Dutch oven, combine meat, tomatoes, tomato sauce, onion, peppers, vinegar and sugar. Combine flour with water and stir until smooth; stir into meat mixture. Add salt, pepper, turmeric, hot sauce and Worcestershire. Bring to a boil, reduce heat and simmer, partly covered, for an hour or until thickened. Taste and adjust seasonings. Add corn and cook 10 minutes more.
Serves 8-10.

OLGA'S VICHYSSOISE

2	tablespoons olive oil
4-5	strips bacon, diced
1	small clove garlic, minced
3	medium onions, chopped
1	bunch leeks, tops and bottoms chopped separately
Freshly ground pepper to taste	
2	medium potatoes, peeled and sliced thin
1	tablespoon flour
1	quart plus ¾ cup chicken stock
1	quart half and half
2	tablespoons butter
Dash hot pepper sauce	

In a large saucepan or Dutch oven over medium heat place oil, bacon, garlic, onions, the tops of the leeks and the pepper. Sauté gently 10 minutes. Add the potatoes and cook 10 minutes longer. Stir in flour. Add 1 quart chicken stock and cream and bring to a boil. Reduce heat and simmer for 10 minutes. Strain through a colander, but do not mash. Return to pot.

Finely chop the bottoms of the leeks. In a small saucepan over medium heat combine remaining ¾ cup chicken stock, butter and the bottoms of the leeks. Simmer gently until the leeks are tender, 8-10 minutes. Add to strained mixture and stir over medium heat to combine. Add hot pepper sauce. Soup may be served hot. To serve chilled, allow to come to room temperature and then refrigerate. Serves 8-10.

ALPINE POTATO SOUP

3	tablespoons butter or margarine
1	cup onion, chopped
½	cup carrot, shredded
3	cups milk
1	cup chicken broth
Salt and pepper to taste	
⅛	teaspoon nutmeg
1	cup instant mashed potato flakes
1	cup Swiss cheese, shredded

In a medium saucepan, melt butter or margarine and sauté onion and carrot until tender. Stir in milk, broth, salt, pepper and nutmeg; bring to a boil. Stir in potato flakes; cook until thickened. Add Swiss cheese; cook and stir until just melted. Serves 4.

ROAST BEEF AND VEGETABLE SOUP

3-3½ pounds beef chuck roast with bone

1 large meaty soup bone

1½ cups potatoes, peeled, cut into 1" cubes

1½ cups frozen baby lima beans or peas

1½ cups celery cut into 1" cubes (include a few leaves)

1½ cups onions, chopped

1½ cups carrots, peeled, cut into 1" cubes

2 cups cabbage, chopped

2 28-ounce cans tomatoes, undrained and chopped

1 cup turnips, peeled, cut into 1" cubes

8 beef bouillon cubes

Salt and pepper to taste

2-3 bay leaves

1 teaspoon oregano, or to taste

Onion salt and celery salt to taste

3-4 sprigs fresh parsley

1 tablespoon sugar

Place beef and bone in a large soup kettle and cover with 2-2½ quarts of cold water. Bring to a boil. Reduce heat and simmer, partially covered, for 30-40 minutes. Add vegetables and seasonings. Simmer for 2-3 hours longer. Remove bones and discard. Cut beef into bite-sized pieces.

Makes 8-10 generous servings.

BUTTERNUT BISQUE

4	cups cooked butternut squash
2	tablespoons butter
1	medium onion, chopped
½	teaspoon curry powder
1	teaspoon Worcestershire sauce
¼	teaspoon nutmeg
1	tablespoon creamy peanut butter
4	cups chicken broth
Salt and pepper to taste	
½	cup half and half

In a skillet over medium heat melt butter, and sauté onion until soft. Place onion and squash in a food processor fitted with a metal blade. Add curry, Worcestershire, nutmeg, peanut butter and one cup of the chicken stock; process all until smooth. Turn mixture into a large saucepan and add the remaining chicken stock, salt and pepper. Bring to a boil, reduce heat and simmer 15 minutes to blend the flavors. Add the cream; do not allow to boil.

Makes 6 servings.

BEER CHEESE SOUP

¾	cup butter
½	cup finely diced celery
½	cup finely diced carrots
½	cup finely diced onion
½	cup flour
½	teaspoon dry mustard
¼	teaspoon Accent
5	cups chicken broth
2	tablespooons Parmesan cheese, grated
6	ounces Cheddar cheese, shredded
1	11-ounce bottle beer
Salt and pepper to taste	

In a Dutch oven or large saucepan, melt butter and sauté vegetables until tender, but not browned. Stir in flour, mustard and Accent; cook 1 minute. Slowly add broth, stirring constantly. Cook 5 minutes, stirring occasionally. Blend in Parmesan, Cheddar and beer. Simmer 10 minutes.
4-6 servings.

POTAGE CHOISI

2 tablespoons butter

1 medium onion, minced

1 leek, including green, minced

4 tablespoons flour

1½ quarts extra rich chicken broth

1 large head Boston lettuce, chopped

¼ - ½ cup cream

1 egg yolk

Salt to taste

White pepper to taste

In soup pot, sauté onion and leek in butter over low heat until soft, being careful to keep white. Add flour and cook several minutes. Add chicken broth and bring to a boil. Add lettuce and boil gently 35-40 minutes. Pureé in blender in small batches. The soup can be made ahead at this point and refrigerated. When ready to serve, bring soup to a boil. Combine cream and egg yolk. Add a small amount of hot soup to mixture, then add mixture to the soup. Do not boil. Season with salt and pepper. Garnish as desired, sprinkle with fresh chopped parsley or serve croutons separately. If desired, top with a dollop of sour cream.
Serves 6.

GREEN AND WHITE SOUP

2	tablespoons unsalted butter
1	cup carrots, peeled and sliced thin
1	cup celery, sliced thin
1	medium onion, chopped
1	clove garlic, minced
1	pound dried white beans, soaked overnight
3	cups chicken stock, canned or homemade
1	bay leaf
1	smoked ham hock
1	16-ounce can tomatoes, drained and chopped
	Freshly ground black pepper to taste
8	ounces spinach fettuccine
½	cup freshly grated Parmesan cheese

Melt the butter in a large kettle. Add the carrots, celery, onion and garlic and cook, covered, over medium-low heat, stirring occasionally for 10 minutes. Add the beans, the chicken stock, bay leaf, ham hock, tomatoes and enough water to cover by 1". Bring to a boil; reduce heat and simmer, partially covered, for 1½ hours. Skim as needed and stir occasionally. Remove ham hock and chop meat. Return meat to the pot. Add salt and pepper to taste, along with the fettucine. Simmer uncovered for 8-10 minutes or until pasta is al dente. Serve with the grated Parmesan cheese.
6-8 servings.

BROCCOLI SOUP

1	medium onion, chopped
1	bunch broccoli, chopped
6	cups chicken broth, canned or homemade
2	cups Cheddar cheese, shredded
3	cups half and half
½	cup sherry (optional)

CREAM SAUCE BASE:

½	cup butter
½	cup flour

Cook onion and broccoli in chicken broth until tender, about 20 minutes. While broccoli cooks, make the cream sauce base. Melt butter in a small skillet over medium heat. Blend in flour, stirring until smooth and cooked, 2-3 minutes. Add cream sauce base to broth and cook for 5 minutes, stirring to blend. Remove from heat, add Cheddar cheese and stir until cheese is melted. Add half and half and the sherry; heat gently, but do not boil.
Makes 8 servings.

TURKEY CHILI

2	tablespoons vegetable oil
1½	cups onion, finely minced
1½	cups red and green pepper, chopped
2	pounds ground turkey
2	cloves garlic, minced
3	tablespoons chili powder
1½	teaspoons ground cumin
1	teaspoon oregano
½	teaspoon black pepper
¾	teaspoon crushed red pepper
2	16-ounce cans kidney beans
2	16-ounce cans tomatoes, undrained
¼	cup red wine vinegar

Sauté onion and peppers in oil until soft. Add ground turkey and cook. Stir in spices and cook until blended. Add beans, tomatoes and vinegar. Bring to a boil; reduce heat and simmer for 1½-2 hours, stirring occasionally.
Makes 8 servings.

BRAZILIAN BLACK BEAN SOUP

2½	pounds ham, bone in
4	cups dried black beans, soaked overnight
3	tablespoons olive oil
4	cups chopped onions
1	cup chopped carrots
½	cup chopped celery
2	cloves garlic, pressed
½	teaspoon ground coriander
⅛	teaspoon cinnamon
½	teaspoon black pepper
¼	teaspoon hot pepper sauce
¼	teaspoon cayenne
1	teaspoon salt
½	teaspoon freshly grated orange rind
3	14-ounce cans beef broth or bouillon
1	cup orange juice, red wine or a combination of the two
½	cup Madeira
½	pound pepperoni, sliced

Place ham in a soup kettle and cover with water. Bring to a boil; reduce heat and simmer for 2 hours. Let ham cool in broth. Skim fat; reserve broth and discard bone. Chop meat and reserve. Drain liquid from beans and cook in fresh water to cover 1½-2 hours or until tender. In a skillet heat oil and sauté onion, carrots, celery and garlic until soft. Add coriander, cinnamon, black pepper, hot pepper sauce, cayenne, orange rind and salt. Stir to blend flavors. Add to beans along with ham broth and bouillon. Simmer 3 hours or until beans are very soft. Purée soup in batches in a food processor fitted with a metal blade. Return purée to the stock pot. Add orange juice, Madeira, pepperoni and reserved ham. Reheat to serving temperature.
Makes 8-10 servings.

FRESH ASPARAGUS SOUP

2	pounds of fresh asparagus, cut into pieces, tips set aside
3	cups chicken broth, homemade or canned
1½	tablespoons shallots, finely chopped
4	tablespoons butter
5	tablespoons flour
3	cups half and half
1	teaspoon curry powder, optional
Salt and pepper to taste	
2	tablespoons dry sherry

In a large saucepan bring chicken broth to a boil; reduce heat. Add asparagus tips to the broth and simmer 2 minutes. Remove tips with a slotted spoon and set aside. Add remaining asparagus pieces and shallots and simmer until asparagus is tender. Purée soup in batches in a food processor fitted with a metal blade. In a large saucepan over medium heat, melt butter; add flour and cook for 3 minutes stirring constantly. Add asparagus purée and half and half along with salt, pepper, curry powder and sherry. Simmer 15 minutes, stirring occasionally. Stir in reserved asparagus tips.
Makes 6-8 servings.

MANHATTAN FISH CHOWDER

⅓	cup olive oil
½	cup onion, chopped
4-5	garlic cloves, minced
3	sprigs of fresh parsley, chopped
1	teaspoon dried basil
1	teaspoon dried oregano
½	teaspoon ground turmeric
1	16-ounce can tomatoes, undrained
⅔	cup dry white wine
1½	pounds cod or haddock, cut into 1" pieces
½	pound bay scallops
1	6½-ounce can minced clams, undrained
Salt and freshly ground pepper to taste	

Heat oil in a Dutch oven over medium heat. Add onion and garlic and sauté until soft. Stir in parsley, basil, oregano, turmeric, tomatoes and wine; simmer 5 minutes. Add fish, scallops and clams and simmer gently, partially covered, until fish is tender, about 20 minutes. Season to taste with salt and pepper.
4 servings.

FRESH HERBED TOMATO SOUP

1	tablespoon olive oil
1	large onion, chopped
2	pounds tomatoes, peeled, seeded and chopped
1	quart chicken broth, homemade or canned
3	tablespoons tomato paste
1	teaspoon dried thyme
2	teaspoons tarragon
1	small bay leaf
Salt and cayenne pepper to taste	

In a large saucepan sauté onion in olive oil until soft, 10 minutes. Stir in tomatoes. Add chicken broth, tomato paste, thyme, tarragon, bay leaf, salt and cayenne. Bring to a boil. Reduce heat and simmer, partially covered, until thickened, 25-30 minutes. Purée in batches in a food processor fitted with a metal blade. Soup may be served hot or chilled.
Makes 4 servings.

GARLIC ZUCCHINI SOUP

2	tablespoons butter
1	medium onion, chopped
4	cups chicken stock, homemade or canned
2	pounds zucchini, sliced thin
½	tablespoon red wine vinegar
4	cloves garlic, pressed
Freshly ground black pepper to taste	
2	potatoes, peeled and sliced thin
1	cup sour cream, for garnish
3	tablespoons green onion tops, chopped

In a large saucepan melt the butter and sauté the onion until soft. Add the stock, zucchini, vinegar, garlic and pepper. Bring to a boil, stirring occasionally. Add the potatoes and simmer covered for 30 minutes. Remove from heat and let cool to room temperature. Purée in a food processor fitted with metal blade.

Soup may be served chilled or hot. Garnish with a dollop of sour cream and the chopped green onion tops.
Makes 6 servings.

MINESTRONE

1	pound navy beans
1	pound salt pork, diced
6	tablespoons olive oil
1	medium onion, chopped
2	cloves garlic, minced
4	slices bacon, diced
3	medium potatoes, diced
3	medium stalks celery, diced
3	small carrots, diced
½	head cabbage, shredded
1	bay leaf
1	teaspoon dried basil
1	tablespoon parsley, chopped
1	tablespoon dried oregano
1	teaspoon salt
½	teaspoon pepper
1	6-ounce can tomato paste
½	cup rice, uncooked
1	cup frozen peas
1	10-ounce package Italian greens beans
2	medium zucchini, sliced

In a large soup kettle bring 12 cups of water to a boil; add beans, remove from heat and let sit one hour. Do not drain. Add salt pork and simmer 1 hour. In a medium skillet sauté onion and garlic in olive oil. Add mixture to the beans. Fry bacon; drain and add to beans, along with potatoes, celery, carrots, cabbage, seasonings, tomato paste, rice, peas, green beans and zucchini. Add 4 cups of water. Simmer, uncovered, until thick, stirring occasionally. In a food processor, fitted with a metal blade, purée ½ to ¾ of the soup. You will need to do this in several batches. Return purée to kettle and heat to serving temperature. Garnish with grated Parmesan if desired. Makes 10-12 servings.

SCALLOP CHOWDER

3	medium potatoes, peeled and cubed
1	carrot, peeled and chopped
1	stalk celery, chopped
1	medium onion, chopped
2	cups chicken stock, canned or homemade
½	teaspoon salt, or to taste
	Freshly ground black pepper to taste
½	teaspoon dried thyme
1	small bay leaf
1	pound bay scallops
½	pound mushrooms, sliced
2	tablespoons butter or margarine
½	cup dry white wine
1	cup heavy cream
1	egg yolk, lightly beaten
	Parsley
	Paprika

Place potatoes, carrots, celery and onion in a large pot. Cover with chicken stock and bring to a boil. Add salt, pepper, thyme and bay leaf. Reduce heat and simmer, covered, until vegetables are tender, about 20 minutes. Remove bay leaf and transfer mixture to a food processor fitted with a metal blade. Process until smooth. Meanwhile, melt butter in a small saucepan. Add mushrooms, and sauté for 5 minutes. Add scallops and wine and cook for one minute. Mix cream with egg yolk and add to scallops. Combine scallop mixture with puréed vegetables and broth. Heat, but do not boil. Serve garnished with chopped parsley and paprika.
Makes 4 servings.

SOUPS

CREAM OF ARTICHOKE SOUP

½	cup green onions, chopped
2	carrots, peeled and sliced
2	stalks celery, chopped
½	cup butter or margarine, divided
½	teaspoon dried thyme
½	teaspoon dried oregano
⅛	teaspoon cayenne pepper
4	cups chicken broth
½	pound mushrooms, sliced
1	14-ounce can artichoke hearts, drained and sliced
3	tablespoons flour
1	cup half and half
Salt and pepper to taste	

In a large saucepan over medium heat sauté onion, carrots and celery in ¼ cup of butter. Add thyme, oregano, cayenne, broth, mushrooms and artichokes. Simmer 20 minutes. In a small skillet over medium low heat, melt remaining ¼ cup butter. Stir in flour and cook until smooth and thickened, 2 minutes. Add to artichoke mixture, stirring to blend. Slowly add half and half. Season with salt and pepper. Cook until soup is thick and thoroughly heated. Do not boil.
Makes 4-6 servings.

COLD STRAWBERRY SOUP

2	cups strawberries, fresh or unsweetened frozen
1	cup yogurt
1	cup skim milk
3	tablespoons brown sugar
1	teaspoon lemon juice
1	teaspoon vanilla
Strawberry slices	

Place all ingredients in a food processor or blender and process until smooth. Serve chilled garnished with strawberry slices.
Serves 4.

CAJUN SHRIMP GUMBO

½ cup vegetable oil

½ cup flour

2 large onions, chopped

3 tablespoons butter

2 10-ounce packages frozen okra, thawed and sliced

2⅔ cups fresh tomatoes, peeled, seeded and chopped

2 green peppers, chopped

4 large cloves garlic, minced

2 tablespoons butter

2½ pounds shrimp, peeled and deveined

2½ quarts chicken broth

1 teaspoon crushed red pepper (optional)

4 teaspoons salt, or to taste

2 bay leaves

2 teaspoons Worcestershire sauce

1 teaspoon ground allspice

½ teaspoon freshly ground black pepper

¼ teaspoon dried thyme

2 tablespoons filé powder

Make a roux. In a small heavy skillet heat oil over medium high heat. Add flour, reduce heat and cook, stirring constantly, until mixture is chocolate brown, 15 minutes. Remove from pan and set aside. In a soup kettle sauté onion in 3 tablespoons of butter until soft. Stir in okra and sauté until tender, 5 minutes more.

Add tomatoes and cook 30 minutes. In a separate saucepan sauté green pepper and garlic in 2 tablespoons of butter for 10 minutes. Add to okra mixture. Add broth and all seasonings except for filé powder. Add the roux. Simmer covered for 2 hours. Add shrimp and cook gently 10-15 minutes. Remove from heat and let stand for 10 minutes. Add filé powder. To serve, place a scoop of cooked rice in a soup bowl and ladle soup over the top. 12 servings.

SALADS

RED AND GREEN SALAD

1	small head bibb lettuce
1	small head red leaf lettuce or radicchio (Italian red lettuce)
1	small head green leaf lettuce
½	pound fresh spinach
½	cup fresh mushrooms, thinly sliced
¼	cup green onions, thinly sliced
⅓	cup toasted walnuts
*¼	cup dried red tart cherries

Rinse, dry, and tear greens into bite size pieces. Chill. Heap mixed greens on individual plates. Ladle dressing over top. Garnish each salad with mushrooms, green onions, walnuts, and cherries.

*Michigan dried red cherries are available in gourmet food stores.

CREAMY RASPBERRY VINAIGRETTE:

¼	cup raspberry vinegar
⅓	cup sugar
¾	cup safflower oil
½	cup heavy cream
*¾	cup raspberry purée

Place sugar and vinegar in blender. With machine running slowly add oil. Whisk in cream and raspberry purée. Serves 8 generously.

*Push 1 10-ounce package defrosted raspberries through sieve.

HEARTS OF PALM & WALNUT SALAD

2 or 3 heads Boston or bibb
    lettuce, washed and dried

8   medium fresh mushrooms,
     sliced

½   red pepper, cut in strips

¾   cup walnuts, coarsely chopped

1   14-ounce can hearts of palm,
    drained

DRESSING:

6   tablespoons olive oil

2   tablespoons wine vinegar

1   tablespoon Dijon mustard

Salt and pepper to taste

Sauté walnuts in small amount of butter or non-stick vegetable spray. Cut hearts of palm into slices. Toss the lettuce, mushrooms, walnuts, red pepper and hearts of palm together. To make dressing — combine olive oil, vinegar, mustard and seasonings in a small jar. Mix well and pour over salad just before serving.
Serves 6-8.

HEARTS OF PALM AND TOMATO SALAD

8   medium size plum tomatoes

½   cup fresh basil leaves, packed

2   14-ounce cans hearts of palm,
    drained

1   cup pitted black olives

½   cup olive oil

3   tablespoons white wine vinegar

1½ teaspoons grated lemon peel

¾   teaspoon salt

½   teaspoon freshly ground black
    pepper

½   teaspoon sugar

Slice each tomato into wedges. Place in bowl with basil leaves. Cut hearts of palm into ½″ diagonal slices. Slice each olive in half. Add olives and hearts of palm to tomatoes. In a small bowl with a wire whisk, mix the olive oil with the next five ingredients. Pour this dressing over tomato mixture.
8 servings.

TWO GARDENS SALAD

1	clove garlic
⅓	cup raspberry vinegar
1	egg yolk
2	teaspoons Dijon mustard
¼	teaspoon crushed thyme
¼	teaspoon salt
⅛	teaspoon black pepper
1	cup vegetable oil
6	cups torn assorted lettuce leaves such as red leaf, bibb, and Boston
½	cup whole pecans
1	5-ounce can sliced water chestnuts, drained
*1 to 2 cups edible flowers: violets, nasturtiums, pansies, or rose petals	

To make dressing: process garlic in food processor or blender. Blend in vinegar, egg yolk, mustard, thyme, salt and pepper. While machine is running, add oil in slow, steady stream and process until thickened. Divide lettuce, pecans, and water chestnuts among 4 plates. Garnish with flowers. Dribble dressing over each portion.
Serves 4.

*Be sure flowers used are edible and washed carefully.

See photo illustration.

SUMMER SALAD WITH TOMATILLO DRESSING

2-3 tomatoes, sliced

½ cup sliced black olives

2 cucumbers, sliced

Mixed salads greens

DRESSING:

½ pound tomatillos

3 tablespoons cilantro

2 tablespoons olive oil

1 teaspoon chervil

1 clove garlic

2 teaspoons lime juice

Salt to taste

Arrange greens on salad plates and top with tomatoes, black olives and cucumbers. To make dressing, place tomatillos on a cookie sheet and bake in a 450 degree oven for 10 minutes. Cool, remove husks and rinse. Put tomatillos and remaining dressing ingredients in a food processor and process until well blended. Chill dressing before using.
4 servings.

SUNSHINE SALAD

Assorted greens

1 cup grapefruit sections

1 avocado, sliced

4 tablespoons pine nuts

10 ounces cooked chicken breast, cut in strips

DRESSING:

⅔ cup salad oil

⅓ cup fresh orange juice

¼ cup sugar

3 tablespoons vinegar

½ teaspoon salt

¼ teaspoon dry mustard

Place salad ingredients in salad bowl. Mix dressing ingredients; stir thoroughly. Chill at least 1 hour before using. Toss and add dressing just before serving.
Serves 4.

CABBAGE SLAW PLUS

1 medium head cabbage, shredded

3 green onions, chopped

2 ounces slivered almonds

½ cup sunflower seeds

1 package chicken noodle oriental soup mix

½ cup vegetable oil

2 tablespoons sugar

Seasoning from soup package

In a 2-quart bowl, combine cabbage, onions, almonds, sunflower seeds and noodles, breaking up noodles. Mix the vegetable oil, sugar, and seasoning in a small bowl and stir well. Pour dressing over other ingredients. Must be made day before serving. Cover tightly, refrigerate, and stir occasionally.
Serves 6-8.

ITALIAN COLE SLAW

1	medium head cabbage, shredded, plus one or more of the following:
1	medium carrot, grated
1	red or green pepper, chopped
1	onion, chopped
½	cup stuffed olives, sliced

Combine ingredients in a large bowl. Pour over the vegetables one of the dressings below. Slaw should be covered and refrigerated for at least 6 hours. Do not stir until ready to serve. Cole slaw keeps well for several days.

DRESSING #1

Put ⅞ cup sugar on top of vegetables

Bring following ingredients to boil:

1	cup vinegar
¾	cup vegetable oil
2	teaspoons sugar
2	teaspoons salt
1	teaspoon dry mustard
1½	teaspoons celery seed

Stir well and pour over cabbage while still hot.

DRESSING #2

1	cup sugar
1	teaspoon salt
½	cup cider vinegar
½	cup honey
½	cup vegetable oil

Bring to boil and pour over cabbage while hot.

DRESSING #3

¼	cup vegetable oil
½	cup sugar
¼	cup water
¼	teaspoon salt

Mix to dissolve sugar. Pour over vegetables and let stand at least 3 hours.
6-8 servings.

SALADS

VIDALIA ONION SALAD

2	medium Vidalia onions, sliced
1	cup water
½	cup sugar
¼	cup white vinegar
1	tablespoon plus 1 teaspoon mayonnaise
1	teaspoon celery seed

Combine water, sugar, vinegar, and stir until sugar is dissolved. Place onion rings in a shallow dish and pour dressing mixture over to cover. Chill 2 hours or more; drain. Stir in mayonnaise and celery seed. Serve on lettuce.
Serves 6-8.

LYDIA'S VEGETABLE SALAD

1	6-ounce package orange gelatin
¾	cup hot water
¾	cup cold water
⅔	cup sour cream
⅓	cup salad dressing
½	tablespoon lemon juice
⅛	teaspoon garlic powder
1	teaspoon dill weed
½	cup grated carrots
¼	cup sliced radishes
¼	cup sliced scallions
¼	cup diced cucumbers (or celery)
¼	cup sliced ripe olives

Pour hot water over gelatin and stir until thoroughly dissolved. Add cold water and stir well. Cool. Mix sour cream and salad dressing together. Add lemon juice, garlic powder, and dill weed. When gelatin begins to thicken, fold it into sour cream mixture. Then fold in vegetables. Pour into 9" square pan lightly brushed with salad oil. Chill until firm. Cut into squares and serve on lettuce. May be made in 5-cup mold.
Serves 8-10.

LA SALADE MONACO

6	medium tomatoes, sliced
Salt	
8	anchovy fillets, drained and cut into small pieces
1	green pepper, thinly sliced
16	black olives
4	tablespoons olive oil
8	fresh basil leaves
Black pepper	
2	hard-cooked eggs, quartered or sliced

Sprinkle tomatoes with salt to taste and arrange on individual plates. Cover with layers of anchovy, green pepper, and olives. Sprinkle with olive oil, a little pepper and the basil. Garnish with the eggs. Serves 4.

SPINACH AND STRAWBERRY SALAD

8	cups spinach, washed and dried
1	pint fresh strawberries (cut up if very large)
½	cup sugar
¼	cup cider vinegar
½	cup vegetable oil
2	tablespoons sesame seeds
¼	teaspoon poppy seeds
1½	teaspoons minced onion
¼	teaspoon paprika

Tear spinach and place in salad bowl or on individual salad plates. Add strawberries. Place sugar, vinegar, oil, sesame seeds, poppy seeds, onion and paprika in blender. Process until dressing is smooth. Pour over spinach and strawberries. Toss gently. Serves 8.

Variation: Sliced papaya, mango or kiwi fruit may be used in combination with strawberries.

BROCCOLI LUNCHEON SALAD

1	large bunch broccoli cut in bite size pieces (include peeled and sliced stems) or
2	bunches broccoli cut in bite size pieces using only flowerets
10	slices bacon, cooked crisp and crumbled
½	medium red onion, chopped
⅔	cup raisins
½	cup sunflower seeds (optional)
½	cup fresh mushrooms, sliced (optional)

DRESSING:

½	cup mayonnaise
½	cup plain yogurt or use
1	cup mayonnaise
¼	cup sugar
2	tablespoons cider vinegar or lemon juice

Mix mayonnaise or mayonnaise/ yogurt with sugar and lemon juice or vinegar. Toss with remaining ingredients. Refrigerate at least 2 hours before serving. Will keep 2 or 3 days in the refrigerator.
Serves 6.

MUSHROOM AND BROCCOLI SALAD

1	pound fresh mushrooms, cleaned and sliced
1	bunch broccoli
½	cup green onions, finely chopped
½	cup sugar
1	teaspoon salt
1	teaspoon paprika
1	teaspoon celery seed
1	teaspoon onion powder
1	cup vegetable oil
¼	cup cider or wine vinegar

Break off flowerets from broccoli and combine with mushrooms and green onions. Put sugar, salt, paprika, celery seed, onion powder, oil, and vinegar in jar with lid. Shake well and let stand for one hour. Pour dressing over the vegetables and stir. Refrigerate at least one hour before serving. Makes 6-8 servings.

BROCCOLI AND PEA SALAD

1	bunch broccoli
2	bunches green onions, chopped
3	10-ounce boxes frozen peas, thawed
1	8-ounce bottle of creamy Caesar or creamy garlic dressing

Wash broccoli and break into small flowerets. Skin the stems with a scraper and chop up. Combine with the chopped green onions and green peas. Toss the dressing with vegetables and let stand overnight in refrigerator. Makes 6-8 servings.

TURKISH BEAN SALAD

3	1-pound cans kidney beans
¾	cup olive oil
2	large onions, chopped
3	large carrots, sliced
1	clove garlic, minced
Juice of 1 lemon	
½	6-ounce can tomato paste
1	teaspoon salt
½	teaspoon celery salt

Drain the beans and save a small amount of the liquid. Sauté the onions, carrots and garlic in olive oil until soft. Add lemon juice, tomato paste, salt and celery salt. Stir in beans with liquid and simmer 1 hour. Serve at room temperature.
10-12 servings.

KIDNEY BEAN AND PEA SALAD

2	15-ounce cans red kidney beans, well-drained
1	15-ounce can of small green peas, drained
6	stalks celery, thinly sliced
2	tablespoons green pickle relish, well-drained
2	cups cooked elbow macaroni
1	cup longhorn cheese, cut into ¼″ cubes
1	cup mayonnaise
¼	teaspoon black pepper, freshly ground
½	small head iceberg lettuce, shredded by hand
2	hard cooked eggs, sliced

Combine all ingredients except the lettuce and eggs. Mound the salad on the shredded lettuce on a large platter. Top with the sliced hard cooked eggs. Refrigerate until serving time. Will keep for 2 days. Makes 10 servings — a complete, nutritious meal.

BRAZILIAN SALAD

4	**ears corn, steamed and kernels cut off cob**
1	**pound kale steamed until just tender; drained and coarsely chopped**
2	**cups cooked brown rice**
1	**15-ounce can black beans, well drained, or 2 cups cooked black beans**
1	**medium sweet onion (Vidalia is best) coarsely chopped (about 1 cup) or green onions with some tops included**
2	**tomatoes, chunked**
½	**red pepper, coarsely chopped, or a 4-ounce jar pimentos chopped**
½	**cup Italian parsley, snipped**
Salt, pepper, red pepper flakes to taste	
4	**tablespoons garlic vinaigrette**

Mix corn kernels, kale, and rice in large bowl using fingers if necessary to distribute kale evenly. Add remaining ingredients and toss well with dressing. Serve at room temperature on crispy greens such as romaine or arugula.
A complete meal for four.

VINAIGRETTE:

2	**large cloves garlic crushed**
½	**teaspoon salt**
¼	**teaspoon dry mustard**
2	**tablespoons red wine vinegar**
½	**cup olive oil**

Mix garlic, salt and mustard into paste. Add vinegar and oil and shake well.

CHICKEN SALAD SUPREME

3	whole boned chicken breasts, cooked
1	8-ounce bottle French dressing
3	stalks celery, diced
1	7½-ounce can pineapple chunks, drained
1	2¾-ounce package blanched almonds
¾	cup green seedless grapes, halved
½	cup mayonnaise
½	cup sour cream
Salt to taste	

Cut chicken into cubes and marinate overnight in French dressing. Drain chicken and combine with celery, pineapple, almonds, and grapes. Add mayonnaise, sour cream and salt to taste and mix thoroughly. Chill until serving time.
Makes 6-8 portions.

SYRIAN SALAD

1	cup bulgur wheat
6	tablespoons fresh lemon juice
3	tablespoons olive or vegetable oil
2	teaspoons salt
½	teaspoon pepper
¼	teaspoon ground allspice
¼	teaspoon cinnamon
1	bunch parsley, snipped (use mostly leaves)
1	cup green onions, finely chopped
4	tomatoes, cubed
3	tablespoons fresh or dried mint leaves, chopped

Wash bulgur wheat 2 or 3 times in cold water. Drain. Pour over it ¼ cup cold water and let stand one hour or until light and puffy. Mix together lemon juice, oil, salt, pepper, allspice, and cinnamon. In medium-sized bowl combine parsley, onions, tomatoes, mint leaves and wheat. Pour dressing over salad and mix well. Chill 1 hour or more before serving. Makes 6-8 portions.

MANDARIN ORANGE SALAD

½	pound romaine washed, drained and torn
½	pound spinach washed, drained and torn
1	medium red onion, sliced
1	medium avocado, sliced
1	cup celery, chopped
1	cup mandarin orange slices, drained
¼	cup sliced almonds, toasted

DRESSING:

1	teaspoon salt
2	tablespoons sugar
2	tablespoons white vinegar
¼	cup olive oil
Dash hot pepper sauce	
1	tablespoon parsley, snipped

Mix together the romaine lettuce, spinach, red onion, avocado, celery and the orange slices. Toss with the dressing. Top with the toasted almonds.

To make the dressing — shake all the listed ingredients in a jar until the sugar dissolves.
4-6 servings.

GERMAN POTATO SALAD

6	medium potatoes, cubed, boiled, and cooled
6	slices bacon, cubed and sautéed until crisp; save drippings
1½	tablespoons all-purpose flour
⅓	cup water
⅓	cup cider vinegar
⅓	cup sugar
½	cup onions, chopped
	Salt and pepper
½	teaspoon celery seed (optional)

Add flour to bacon drippings; stir until smooth. Add water, vinegar, and sugar. Simmer 5 minutes. Add cubed, boiled cold potatoes. Heat through; add raw chopped onions, salt, pepper and celery seed. This salad will be juicy. It is delicious a day old, cold.
Serves 6-8.

POTATO SALAD RING

	In large bowl mix:
1	envelope instant onion soup mix
¾	cup mayonnaise
1	tablespoon white vinegar
1	tablespoon sugar
¼	teaspoon black pepper
	Add:
4	cups cooked potatoes, cubed
½	pound salami, cut into ½″ cubes
½	pound Swiss cheese, shredded
4	hard-cooked eggs, chopped
½	cup celery, chopped

Mix well and pack into oiled 6-cup mold. Chill for 3 hours or more and unmold on lettuce. Garnish with parsley, olives, or cherry tomatoes as desired.
Serves 8.

MUSTARD DILL POTATO SALAD

2	pounds new red potatoes, unpeeled
½	cup celery, finely chopped
⅓	cup red onion, finely chopped
3	hard-cooked eggs, chopped
½	cup chopped fresh dill
½	cup mayonnaise
1	tablespoon white vinegar
1	tablespoon Dijon mustard
Salt and freshly ground pepper	
Lettuce	
Cherry tomatoes	

Scrub potatoes and cut into large chunks. Place in a saucepan and cover with salted water. Cover and bring to a boil; reduce heat and cook until tender, about 15 minutes. Drain and transfer to a large bowl. Cool. Add celery, onion, hard-cooked eggs and dill to potatoes and toss. Combine mayonnaise, vinegar and mustard. Add to potatoes and toss. Season with salt and pepper to taste. Serve on a bed of lettuce and garnish with cherry tomatoes.
Serves 6.

ROASTED POTATO SALAD

2½	pounds small red or Yukon Gold potatoes
1	garlic clove, chopped
5	tablespoons olive oil
1½	tablespoons red wine vinegar
1	tablespoon grainy mustard
2	teaspoons minced chives
1	teaspoon fresh rosemary or ¾ teaspoon dried rosemary
Salt and pepper (optional)	

Preheat oven to 425 degrees. Scrub potatoes and cut in bite-size pieces. Place them in a single layer in 2 quart baking dish. Sprinkle garlic, 3 tablespoons oil, salt and pepper over the potatoes and toss. Roast for 30 to 40 minutes. Rearrange every 10 minutes.

Beat vinegar and mustard in serving bowl. Whisk in remaining 2 tablespoons olive oil until dressing is smooth. Add roasted potatoes and mix gently. Cool to room temperature. Just before serving, fold in chives and rosemary.
Serves 6.

TAFFY APPLE SALAD

1	20-ounce can chunk pineapple
2	cups mini marshmallows
1	tablespoon all-purpose flour
½	cup sugar
1½	tablespoons white vinegar
1	egg well beaten
1	8-ounce carton non-dairy whipped topping
2	cups unpeeled diced apples
1½	cups salted peanuts

Drain juice from pineapple and save. Combine pineapple chunks and marshmallows; refrigerate overnight. Mix juice, flour, sugar, vinegar and well-beaten egg. Cook until thick; refrigerate overnight.

Next day combine whipped topping with pineapple-marshmallow mixture. Combine with apples and peanuts. Mix with cooked dressing. Reserve a few peanuts; chop and sprinkle on top when transferred to serving bowl. 8 servings.

MOLDED BEET SALAD

1	3-ounce package raspberry gelatin
1	cup boiling water
½	cup sugar
¼	cup beet juice
¼	cup vinegar
2	teaspoons horseradish
¼	cup sour cream
1	16-ounce can shoestring beets, well drained, juice reserved

Dissolve gelatin in boiling water in medium bowl. Add sugar, beet juice, vinegar, horseradish, and sour cream. Stir until smooth and well blended. Add the beets. Pour into a 9" x 9" glass dish and chill until firm. Cut in squares and serve on lettuce.
Serves 8-9.

LIME APPLESAUCE MOLD

2 pounds applesauce
2 3-ounce packages lime gelatin
1 4-ounce can crushed pineapple with syrup
1 12-ounce can or bottle lemon-lime carbonated beverage

Combine applesauce and gelatin in saucepan. Cook and stir over medium heat until gelatin dissolves. Cool to room temperature. Fold in pineapple and syrup. Gently stir in carbonated beverage. Turn into oiled mold and chill. Unmold and serve plain or garnished with mandarin orange slices.
Makes 10-12 servings.

HOLIDAY FREEZE

Blend in blender:
2 3-ounce packages cream cheese
2 tablespoons mayonnaise
2 tablespoons sugar
Place cheese mixture in large mixing bowl. Add:
1 16-ounce can whole cranberry sauce
1 9-ounce can (1 cup) crushed pineapple (drained)
½ cup chopped ripe olives
½ cup chopped celery
½ cup walnuts or pecans (broken or chopped)
Fold in:
1 cup heavy cream, whipped

Freeze for 6 hours or overnight. Remove from freezer 15 minutes before serving. Use 8" x 4" x 3" pan.
Serves 10.

ZIPPY PINEAPPLE SALAD

1	3-ounce package lemon gelatin
1	3-ounce package lime gelatin
2	cups boiling water
1	cup evaporated milk
1	pound cottage cheese
½	cup mayonnaise
3	tablespoons prepared horseradish
1	20-ounce can crushed pineapple, drained

Dissolve gelatin in boiling water. Add milk, cheese, mayonnaise, horseradish and pineapple. Stir well and pour into 10" mold. Chill until set. Unmold and serve on lettuce or with fruit garnishes of your choice.
Serves 8.

CRANBERRY MOLD

1	16-ounce can cranberry jelly
3	tablespoons lemon juice
1	cup heavy cream
¼	cup confectioners sugar
¼	cup mayonnaise
1	cup walnuts, chopped

Line muffin tin with papers. Mix cranberry jelly and lemon juice well and place in paper cups. Fill cups about half full. Beat cream until thick; fold in sugar, mayonnaise and walnuts. Put this mixture over cranberry jelly and lemon juice. Place in freezer until serving time. Makes 12-14 servings.

CRANBERRY RELISH

4½	cups fresh cranberries, washed
2	large tart apples, pared
2	large oranges, quartered with seeds removed
2	cups sugar

Coarsely chop apples, cranberries and oranges in food processor. Place in large bowl and stir in sugar. Let stand overnight in refrigerator. Serve cold.
Makes about 3½ cups.

CELERY SEED DRESSING

1	cup sugar
1	tablespoon dry mustard
1	teaspoon salt
¾	cup vinegar
1	cup vegetable oil
1	tablespoon celery seed
1	onion, cut in chunks
2	cloves garlic, cut up

Process all ingredients in blender until well mixed. Store in refrigerator in covered glass jar.
Makes about 3 cups.

HONEY MUSTARD SALAD DRESSING

1 pint mayonnaise
1 cup prepared mustard
⅓ cup honey
4 tablespoons brown sugar
3-4 tablespoons lemon juice
⅛ cup onion, finely chopped
1 tablespoon poppy seeds
Dash Worcestershire sauce
Dash hot pepper sauce

Mix all ingredients together in food processor, blender or jar. Mix very well. Store in refrigerator.
Makes about 3½ cups.

SOUTHWEST DRESSING

2 cups mayonnaise
1 avocado, mashed
8 green onions, chopped
1 ounce anchovies, chopped
4 tablespoons buttermilk
1 teaspoon hot pepper sauce
½ teaspoon dry mustard
¼ teaspoon pepper
1½ tablespoons white Worcestershire sauce
1½ tablespoons soy sauce
2 teaspoons wine vinegar
1 tablespoon fresh lemon juice
¼ teaspoon celery seed
¼ teaspoon oregano
1 clove garlic, crushed

Mix all ingredients thoroughly and chill well before serving.
Makes 4 cups.

SALADS

GARLIC CHEESE SALAD DRESSING

3 cloves garlic, crushed
2 tablespoons Parmesan cheese, grated
¼ teaspoon pepper
½ teaspoon salt
2 tablespoons honey
Dash of cayenne pepper
⅔ cup olive oil
⅓ cup red wine vinegar
1 teaspoon lemon juice
1 teaspoon oregano

Put all ingredients in blender, blend until smooth.
Makes 1¼ cups.

CAESAR DRESSING

2 cups salad oil
2 eggs, beaten
1 tablespoon salt
6 cloves garlic, chopped very fine
2 lemons, squeezed
1 tablespoon pepper
1 cup Parmesan cheese, grated
1 tablespoon white Worcestershire sauce

Combine beaten eggs and ¼ cup oil. Add remaining oil and lemon juice to egg mixture. Combine garlic and salt together, stir into oil mixture and add remaining ingredients. Chill well. Serve on romaine lettuce.
Makes 3 cups.

NO YOLK MAYONNAISE

2	large egg whites, room temperature
2	teaspoons Dijon style mustard
1	teaspoon red wine vinegar
¼	teaspoon salt
⅛	teaspoon white pepper
1½	cups vegetable oil, or ¾ cup extra virgin olive oil

In a blender, mix egg whites, mustard, vinegar, salt, pepper and 3 tablespoons oil on medium speed for 1 minute. Then with the machine running, add the remaining oil, in a thin steady stream. The mixture will thicken slowly as the oil is added. Pour into a 1½ cup glass container. Cover and refrigerate. Will keep for 3 weeks. Stir before serving.

BREADS

HERBED BREAD

3	cups warm water - divided
1	teaspoon sugar
¼	teaspoon ginger
2	packages dry yeast
7-8	cups flour - divided
2	tablespoons sugar
3	teaspoons powdered chicken stock
1	teaspoon thyme
1	teaspoon summer savory
1	teaspoon rosemary
2	teaspoons salt
½	cup softened butter or margarine

In a small bowl combine ½ cup warm water, 1 teaspoon sugar, ginger, and yeast. Let stand 5 minutes or until it bubbles. In a large bowl stir 2 cups warm water, 2 tablespoons sugar and 3 cups of flour. Add powdered chicken stock that has been dissolved in ½ cup warm water. Mix. Add yeast mixture and beat 1 minute. Add the herbs and salt. Stir in the softened butter and 4 more cups of flour. Mix thoroughly. Spread ½ cup flour on board and knead this into the dough. The dough will start out a little sticky and hard to handle. Keep kneading until dough is elastic, about 7-8 minutes. Put into a buttered bowl, turning to butter the top. Cover and let rise until doubled, about 1 hour. Make 2 loaves and let rise in greased pans (9" x 5" x 3") until dough comes to top of pans, about 45 minutes. Bake in preheated 350 degree oven for 50 minutes.

SWEDISH RYE BREAD

4	cups medium rye flour (sift into large bowl or Dutch oven)
1	cup white sugar
½	cup brown sugar
2	teaspoons salt
3½	cups warm potato water*
3	tablespoons molasses
1	yeast cake, melted in ½ cup cold water
½	cup shortening
6	cups white flour, divided (4 cups and 2 cups)

Stir the first 7 ingredients together. Cover bowl tightly and wrap in towel. Place in warm place to double in size, about 2 hours. After dough has doubled, add ½ cup shortening and 4 cups white flour. Knead and stir dough until it forms a weighty solid mass in bottom of bowl. Shape dough in a smooth form; cover and wrap bowl in a towel and put in a warm place to rise a second time. When dough has doubled in size, about an hour, add 2 cups white flour. Knead the dough, either in bowl or on a surface dusted with flour. Divide dough into three equal parts and place dough into 3 greased bread pans (loaf size). Place pans of dough in a warm spot, cover with a towel and let dough double in size the third time. Bake at 375 degrees for 30-40 minutes.

*Note: Water reserved from boiling 6 potatoes.

SCONES

2	cups flour
3	tablespoons sugar
1	tablespoon baking powder
Dash of salt	
½	cup butter, unsalted
2	large eggs
½	cup skim milk
Buttered parchment paper (not necessary but scones brown better on bottom)	

EGG WASH:

2	eggs
¼	cup skim milk

Preheat oven to 450 degrees. Sift flour, sugar, baking powder and salt together. Cut in butter, add eggs and milk. Blend lightly. Place on floured board and gently knead. Roll out ¾" thick. Cut into circles using cookie cutter. Place on buttered parchment paper on cookie sheet. Mix egg wash and brush scones. Bake for 15-20 minutes.
Makes 24 scones.

Variations: Add ¼ cup chopped dried apricots, raisins or pecans and serve at breakfast. Reduce sugar to 1 tablespoon and flavor dough with dried dill or Romano cheese. After baking and cooling, split and spread with ham or turkey and serve as appetizers.

HOT HORN ROLLS

2	packages dry yeast
1	cup lukewarm water
½	cup sugar
½	cup margarine
3	eggs, beaten
1	teaspoon salt
5	cups flour

Add yeast to water, set aside. Cream sugar and margarine, add eggs and yeast mixture. Add salt and flour, mix well. Refrigerate overnight.

Divide dough into 4 sections. Roll each section into a large circle about ¼" thick. Cut each section into 16 wedge-shaped pieces, and roll wide end up into little horns. Let stand in warm place uncovered for 1 hour.

Bake in preheated 400 degree oven for 10-15 minutes on greased cookie sheets. Remove when golden brown and brush with melted butter. Makes 5-6 dozen.

THANKSGIVING BUNS

4½ cups all purpose flour

2 packages dry yeast

¾ cup warm water

2 teaspoons baking powder

1¼ teaspoons salt

¼ cup sugar

½ cup margarine or butter

*1¼ cup buttermilk

Heat oven to 350 degrees; turn off and let cool 10 minutes. Place flour in warm oven for 15 minutes. Dissolve yeast in warm water. Place heated flour, baking powder, salt and sugar in a large bowl. Cut in margarine until mixture looks like cornmeal. Make a "well" in the center, add buttermilk and yeast. Stir; then knead in bowl to blend well. Add more flour as necessary until dough does not adhere to bowl. Dough should be soft and slightly sticky. Knead 2 minutes. Cover and let rise 1 hour or until doubled in bulk. Punch down and divide into 24 equal pieces. Shape each piece into a smooth ball and place on an oiled cookie sheet. Cover and let rise until doubled, about 45 minutes.

Bake in preheated 375 degree oven for 15-20 minutes. To freeze, cool and wrap in foil. Heat at 350 degrees for 20 minutes.

*You can use 1¼ cups sweet milk and 1 tablespoon and a scant teaspoon of vinegar in place of the buttermilk.

BREADS

POPOVERS

1	cup flour
¼	teaspoon salt
1	tablespoon melted butter or margarine
1	cup milk, room temperature
2	eggs, room temperature

Oil the popover pans and place in a preheated 450 degree oven for 5-8 minutes. In a mixing bowl, sift flour and salt. Combine melted butter and milk, stir into the flour mixture; mix thoroughly. Batter should be smooth. Add eggs, one at a time, to the batter, beating until just mixed. Pour the batter into the hot cups, about ⅔ full.

Bake at 450 degrees for 15 minutes, reduce heat to 350 degrees and continue baking another 10-15 minutes. Popovers should be brown and crisp on the outside. Puncture with a toothpick to let steam out.
Makes 1 dozen.

See photo illustration.

KRASL COUNTRY KITCHEN BEER BREAD

3	cups self-rising flour
3	tablespoons sugar
1	can beer
1	tablespoon butter

In a glass bowl using a wooden spoon, mix the flour, sugar and beer. Batter will be lumpy. Pour into two 7" x 3" pans or one 9" x 5" x 3" pan. Dot top with butter. Bake at 350 degrees for 40 minutes. Bake longer if larger pan is used. Recipe cannot be doubled.

BRIOCHE

1	cup milk
½	cup butter or margarine
1	teaspoon salt
½	cup sugar
2	packages active dry yeast
¼	cup warm water (110 to 115 degrees)
4	eggs, beaten
1	teaspoon grated lemon peel
5	cups sifted all-purpose flour
Melted butter	

Scald milk, stir in ½ cup butter, salt and sugar. Cool to lukewarm. Sprinkle yeast on warm water, stirring to dissolve.

Combine eggs and lemon peel. Add to milk mixture. Stir in yeast. Beat in flour, a little at a time, to make a soft dough. Turn onto floured board; knead lightly until dough is smooth and satiny. Place in a greased bowl, turning dough over to grease top. Cover and let rise in a warm place until doubled, about 2 hours. Punch down and turn out on floured board. Knead lightly. Shape ⅔ of the dough into smooth balls about 2 inches in diameter. Shape remaining dough in 1 inch balls. Place large balls in greased muffin pan cups. Flatten balls slightly. Make a deep indentation in each with finger or handle of a wooden spoon; shape small balls like teardrops and set one firmly in the indentation in each ball in muffin pan cups. Brush with melted butter. Cover and let rise until doubled, about 1 hour. Bake in 425 degree oven about 10 minutes. Remove from pans at once and cool on wire racks. Serve warm or wrap cold rolls in aluminum foil and heat in oven a few minutes before serving.
Makes 3 dozen rolls.

REFRIGERATOR ROLLS

1	cup boiling water
1	cup scalded milk
½	cup butter
1½	teaspoon salt
Scant ½ cup sugar	
2	eggs
1	package dry yeast (not quick-rising yeast)
½	cup lukewarm water
7¼-7½ cups unbleached all purpose flour	

Put butter, sugar and salt into a mixing bowl. Add boiling water and scalded milk. Stir to dissolve the sugar. Cool to lukewarm. Beat eggs, add to mixture. Dissolve yeast in ½ cup lukewarm water, then add to mixture. Add 2-3 cups flour and beat thoroughly. Add the remaining flour. (This is a thick mixture and will take a heavy duty beater to mix it.) Mix thoroughly; this takes the place of kneading.

Lightly butter the top of the dough, smoothing the top; this prevents crusting. Cover tightly and place in the refrigerator at least 4-5 hours. When ready to bake, roll dough out to ¼" thickness and form into clover leaf or parker house rolls. Bake at 400 degrees for 10-12 minutes. This recipe makes 2 to 2½ dozen rolls. May make a day ahead and refrigerate overnight.

LINDA'S CHEESE BREAD

1	loaf poppy seed French bread
1	cup butter or margarine
8	ounces Swiss cheese slices, cut into triangles
2	tablespoons minced onions
1	tablespoon prepared mustard

Slash the top of the bread approximately every 3". Place loaf on a sheet of foil, large enough to wrap it. Stuff the slashes with the cheese slices. Melt butter and add onion and mustard. Pour sauce over bread, then wrap in foil and bake at 350 degrees for 30 minutes.

CHILI CORN BREAD

1½	cups corn kernels, uncooked
1	cup yellow cornmeal
3	teaspoons double-acting baking powder
1	cup sour cream
¼	cup melted butter or margarine
2	eggs, beaten
¼	pound Swiss cheese, diced
1	can peeled green chilies, drained and chopped

Combine all ingredients in order listed. Pour into a well greased 9-inch square baking pan. Bake 1 hour in a preheated 350 degree oven.
Serves 6.

STRAWBERRY NUT BREAD

3	cups all purpose flour
1	teaspoon baking soda
½	teaspoon salt
3	teaspoons cinnamon
2	cups sugar, plus 2 tablespoons (reserve 2 tablespoons)
2-3	cups sliced fresh strawberries — don't try frozen berries
4	eggs
1¼	cups vegetable oil
1	cup chopped nuts

Sift dry ingredients into a large bowl. Beat strawberries, oil and eggs together. Pour into dry ingredients and stir just enough to moisten. Stir in nuts and pour into well greased baking pans. Make 2 large loaves in 9" x 5" x 3" pans. Fill half full. Sprinkle with 2 tablespoons sugar. Bake in a preheated 350 degree oven for 45-60 minutes or until a toothpick inserted in the center comes out clean. Cool 30 minutes on a rack before removing from pans. Do not slice until cool. Bread is best when wrapped in plastic and refrigerated overnight. Freezes well up to 4 months. Very good with cream cheese with crushed strawberries in it.

DATE NUT BREAD

1½	cups dates, chopped
½	cup nuts, chopped
1	cup hot water
1⅔	cups all purpose flour, sifted
1	teaspoon soda
⅓	cup graham flour
¾	cup brown sugar, firmly packed
¼	cup margarine
½	teaspoon salt
1	egg

Combine dates, nuts and hot water. Let stand. Sift flour, soda, and graham flour three times. Cream brown sugar, margarine and salt thoroughly. Add egg and mix well. Add the date mixture to creamed mixture blending well. Add flour mixture; blend until thoroughly mixed.

Pour batter into a greased 9 x 5 x 3" loaf pan. Bake in a preheated 350 degree oven for 60-70 minutes. Keeps well — may be frozen.

GLAZED LEMON BREAD

1	cup sugar
½	cup margarine
2	eggs
1½	cups flour
1	teaspoon baking powder
½	teaspoon salt
½	cup milk
1	cup chopped nuts

Grated rind of 1 lemon

GLAZE:

Juice of 1 lemon

¼	cup confectioners sugar

Cream sugar, margarine and eggs together. Add remaining ingredients and mix well. Pour into an oiled loaf pan — 8" x 5" x 3". Bake at 325 degrees for 1 hour and 15 minutes. While hot, pierce top of loaf at ½" intervals with a fork or skewer. Pour glaze mixture over the top of the loaf so that it soaks the entire loaf. Let cool in pan. Remove and slice.

SESAME CRACKERS

5	cups all purpose flour
1	envelope quick rise yeast
2	teaspoons salt
¾	teaspoon sugar
¼	cup butter, melted
1¼	cups very warm water (120 degrees - 130 degrees)
1	cup sesame seeds

Combine flour, yeast, salt and sugar in mixing bowl. Blend the butter with 1 cup water, and gradually add to dry ingredients, beating continuously. Add more water if dough seems too dry. Continue beating dough until it is smooth and elastic. Place in a greased bowl, turning to coat surface. Cover with plastic wrap and a hot damp towel. Let rise in a warm place until doubled in bulk — about ½ hour.

Preheat oven to 375 degrees. Divide dough into 9 equal pieces. Spread sesame seeds on countertop. Place one dough piece on counter at a time and roll as thinly as possible. Place 3 pieces on each cookie sheet and bake on lowest rack 10-15 minutes or until golden brown. Cool on racks. Wrap in plastic or foil, and store in a dry area.

See photo illustration.

SPOON BREAD

1	cup cornmeal
½	cup all purpose flour
¼	cup sugar
1½	teaspoons salt
2	teaspoons baking powder
3	eggs, beaten
2	cups milk
¼	cup butter
1	cup milk

Combine dry ingredients. Stir in eggs and 2 cups milk. Melt butter in a 1½ quart baking dish. Preheat oven to 375 degrees. Pour batter into baking dish then pour 1 cup milk over the top. Bake 45 minutes. Bread should be crusty but soft on the inside. Spoon onto a plate and serve with butter.
Serves 8-10.

PUNCHKINS

2 packages yeast dissolved in ¼ cup warm water

1½ cups milk

½ cup sugar

3 eggs, beaten

5½ cups flour

1¼ teaspoon salt

1 teaspoon vanilla

½ cup white raisins

4-5 cups vegetable oil

Dissolve yeast in lukewarm water. Set aside. Heat milk to scalding; pour into bowl, add sugar and beaten eggs. Add yeast, stir in flour that has been sifted with salt. Add vanilla and raisins. Cover and let rise in a floured bowl until doubled in bulk. Punch dough down and let rise again.

In a medium size saucepan heat 4-5 cups vegetable oil to 375 degrees. Drop batter by irregular spoonfuls into hot oil and cook about 3 minutes, turning to brown on all sides. Drain on heavy paper until cool. (Irregular spoonfuls makes each punchkin a different shape.) Roll in granulated sugar. Store in airtight container. Best if eaten immediately.
Makes 5-6 dozen.

Note from contributor: "My grandmother set her dough on a heating pad and covered the bowl with her handmade afghan!"

CHINESE FLAT BREAD

3	tablespoons sesame seeds
2	cups unbleached all-purpose flour
¾	cup boiling water
4	strips bacon
2-3	green onions, thinly sliced
¼-⅓	cup peanut oil for frying

Heat a small skillet over medium-high heat. Add sesame seeds and toast, stirring constantly until lightly browned (1-2 minutes). Pour into a small bowl immediately and set aside.

Place flour in a food processor fitted with a metal blade. Pour in boiling water and process until dough forms a ball (30 seconds). Turn dough onto a floured board and knead until smooth and elastic (4-5 minutes). Dough can also be mixed and kneaded entirely by hand; increase time to 8 minutes. Cover with a towel and let rest for 15 minutes.

While the dough rests, cook the bacon until crisp, crumble and reserve drippings. On a floured board, roll dough into a circle ½" thick. Brush the surface with the bacon drippings. Sprinkle with the bacon, green onion and ½ of the sesame seeds. Roll the dough into a cylinder; twist and form into a coil. Flatten the coil slightly and press remaining sesame seeds into both sides. Roll into a 10" - 12" circle. (At this point dough may be refrigerated, covered with plastic, up to 3 hours.)

To cook, heat peanut oil in a heavy non-stick skillet over medium-high heat. Place dough in pan and fry until golden, turning several times to cook on both sides.
6 servings.

MANGO CHUTNEY BREAD

2½ cups flour

1 cup firmly packed brown sugar

1 tablespoon baking powder

1 teaspoon salt

3 tablespoons butter or margarine, melted

1¼ cups milk

1 egg, beaten

1½ tablespoons freshly grated orange peel

1 9-10 ounce jar mango chutney

1 cup chopped pecans

Preheat oven to 350 degrees and grease a 9" x 5" loaf pan. Combine flour, brown sugar, baking powder, salt, butter, milk, egg, and orange peel in a large bowl. Fold in chutney and nuts. Pour into prepared loaf pan and bake until tester is clean, 1 hour 15 minutes. Cool bread in pan 10 minutes; turn onto a wire rack to cool completely. Serve with a cream cheese spread.

CURRIED SPREAD:

1 8-ounce package cream cheese, softened

1 tablespoon sugar

2 teaspoons curry powder

Mix the cheese and seasonings and chill. Bring to room temperature to serve.

PEACH SPREAD:

1 8-ounce package cream cheese, softened

½ cup peach preserves

Mix cream cheese and preserves and chill. Bring to room temperature to serve.

BOSTON BAKED BREAD

1	cup sifted all purpose flour
1	teaspoon baking powder
1	teaspoon baking soda
1	teaspoon salt
1	cup cornmeal
1	cup whole wheat flour
1	cup raisins (optional)
¾	cup molasses
2	cups buttermilk or sour milk

Sift together all-purpose flour, baking powder, baking soda and salt in a mixing bowl. Stir in cornmeal, whole wheat flour and raisins. Combine molasses and buttermilk. Stir into dry ingredients and mix thoroughly. Pour into 4 well oiled #2 cans. (These cans usually contain 1-pound, 4-ounces fruit.) Fill ⅔ full or a little less. Cover cans with double thickness of plastic wrap and fasten in place with rubber band.

Place on rack in kettle with tight fitting lid. Add hot water to reach about halfway up the cans. Cover kettle and steam 3 hours. Remove from kettle, uncover cans and place in a very hot oven (450 degrees) for 5 minutes. Remove bread from cans. (Cut out the end of can and push out.) Slice with a heavy thread drawn around the loaf, crossing ends. Cutting hot bread with a knife may make a gummy slice. Serve hot.
Makes 4 loaves.

MONKEY BREAD

1	tablespoon sugar
1	envelope dry yeast
½	cup warm water (110 degrees)
2	cups milk, scalded
1	cup unsalted butter
2	teaspoons salt
6	cups sifted bread flour
3	eggs, room temperature, beaten

Oil large bowl and set aside.

Sprinkle sugar and yeast over water in small cup and stir until dissolved. Combine scalded milk, ¼ cup butter and salt in another large bowl and mix well. Let cool to 110 degrees. Stir in yeast mixture. Add 4 cups flour with eggs and beat until well blended. Add remaining flour and knead briskly until dough is smooth and elastic, about 10 minutes. Rub hands with small amount of oil. Form dough into a ball. Lightly coat top of dough with oil. Transfer to prepared bowl. Cover and let stand until doubled in bulk, about 2 hours. Punch dough down; knead in bowl 2 minutes. Turn dough out onto a lightly floured surface or pastry cloth. Pat or roll to 1″ thickness. Cut dough into 1″ squares.

Melt remaining ¾ cup butter. Cool to 85 degrees. Dip each square of dough into melted butter. Arrange dough in large angel food cake pan (without removable bottom). Cover with oiled wax paper and let stand until doubled in bulk, about 1½ hours.

Position rack in center of oven and preheat to 400 degrees. Bake bread about 35 minutes or until tester comes out clean. If the top begins to brown too quickly, cover pan loosely with foil. Invert onto rack and let cool at least 30 minutes before serving.
Serves 16.

RHUBARB BREAD

1½ cups brown sugar	Combine sugar, flour, soda and salt. Add to egg, oil, and milk which have been well beaten. Mix well. Fold in rhubarb, lemon extract, lemon rind and nuts. Pour into 2 small loaf pans or a 10" tube pan. Sprinkle topping on top. Bake in a preheated 350 degree oven for 55-60 minutes.

1½ cups brown sugar

2½ cups all purpose flour

1 teaspoon baking soda

1 teaspoon salt

1 egg

⅔ cup vegetable oil

1 cup buttermilk or sour milk

1½ cups uncooked rhubarb, cut up

1 teaspoon lemon extract

1 teaspoon lemon rind, grated

½ cup chopped nuts

TOPPING:

½ cup sugar

¼ cup chopped nuts

1 tablespoon margarine

Dash cinnamon

Combine sugar, flour, soda and salt. Add to egg, oil, and milk which have been well beaten. Mix well. Fold in rhubarb, lemon extract, lemon rind and nuts. Pour into 2 small loaf pans or a 10" tube pan. Sprinkle topping on top. Bake in a preheated 350 degree oven for 55-60 minutes.

CRUSTY COUNTRY BREAD

1	envelope dry yeast
⅓	cup warm water (105 degrees to 115 degrees)
4	cups hard wheat white flour
2	teaspoons sugar (optional)
2	teaspoons salt
1¼	cups warm water (120 degrees to 130 degrees)

Lightly oil large bowl; set aside. Stir yeast into ⅓ cup water and let stand until mixture bubbles, about 5-7 minutes. Combine with flour in mixing bowl. Begin beating, adding sugar, salt and remaining water, and continue beating until well mixed. Turn dough out onto a lightly floured board and knead until smooth and elastic, about 5 minutes. Place in greased bowl, turning to coat entire surface. Cover with plastic wrap and hot damp towel and let stand in warm place until almost tripled in volume. When dough has risen, transfer to board, punch down and knead about 2 minutes to eliminate any air bubbles. Return to bowl, cover and let rise again until at least doubled.

Preheat oven to 425 degrees. Grease baking sheet. On a lightly floured board, punch dough down, roll into oval, then form into desired shape. Make several slashes diagonally across top with knife or scissors. Place on a baking sheet and let rise until loaf is doubled. Bake 30 minutes. Reduce heat to 375 degrees and bake 5-10 minutes more for baguettes or 15 minutes more for a single loaf until golden brown and bread gives a hollow sound when tapped on the bottom. Cool on rack.
Makes 2 baguettes or 1 long or round loaf.

See photo illustration.

PUMPKIN MUFFINS

1	cup raisins
½	cup water
2	eggs
1¼	cups sugar
1½	cups canned pumpkin
1	teaspoon cinnamon
1	teaspoon cloves
½	teaspoon salt
⅓	cup vegetable oil
1¾	cups flour
1½	teaspoons baking powder
½	teaspoon baking soda

Soak raisins in water, do not drain. In a large mixing bowl, beat eggs; stir in pumpkin. Add sugar, cloves, cinnamon, and salt. Mix well. Add oil and mix again.

Stir flour, baking powder and baking soda together. Add ½ to the pumpkin mixture. Then add ½ of the raisin mixture. Stir to blend. Add remaining flour and raisin mixture.

Bake in a preheated 400 degree oven for 25 minutes in oiled muffin tins filled ⅔ full.
Makes 16-18 muffins.

BANANA BRAN MUFFINS

1	cup whole bran cereal
¾	cup milk
1	cup flour
½	cup wheat germ
2	teaspoons baking powder
½	teaspoon salt
½	teaspoon cinnamon
6	tablespoons honey
2	tablespoons vegetable oil
¾	cup mashed banana
1	egg
½	cup raisins, optional
½	cup chopped nuts, optional

Preheat oven to 375 degrees. Grease a muffin tin or line with paper baking cups. In a medium bowl combine cereal with milk; set aside. In a large bowl combine flour, wheat germ, baking powder, salt and cinnamon, mixing well. To the cereal mixture add honey, oil, banana and egg. Stir in raisins and nuts, if desired. Blend the cereal mixture well and stir into the flour mixture all at once. Stir only until dry ingredients are well moistened. Fill muffin tins ⅔ full and bake for 15-20 minutes. Serve warm.
Yield: 12 muffins.

BLUEBERRY MUFFINS

1½	cups flour
¾	cup sugar
2	teaspoons baking powder
¼	teaspoon salt (optional)
1	egg
½	cup milk
1½	teaspoons lemon extract
¼	cup vegetable oil
1½	cups fresh or frozen blueberries

Sift flour, sugar, baking powder and salt together. Beat egg, milk and extract together. Fold liquid mixture into dry ingredients. Stir in oil and blueberries gently; do not beat. Preheat oven to 400 degrees. Bake in greased muffin pans for 20-25 minutes.
Makes 20 small muffins.

BREADS

SIMPLY DELICIOUS AND NUTRITIOUS MUFFINS

3	cups whole bran cereal
1	cup boiling water
½	cup vegetable oil
2	eggs
2	tablespoons molasses
2½	cups flour
1	cup raisins
1½	cups sugar
2½	teaspoons baking soda
1½	teaspoons cinnamon
2	cups buttermilk
*½	cup grated carrot
*1	cup chopped nuts
*½	cup dried apricots
*½	cup prunes
*½	cup dates
*½	cup figs
*½	cup shredded coconut
*OPTIONAL INGREDIENTS	

Preheat oven to 400 degrees. Combine cereal and water; stir in oil, eggs and molasses. Add flour, raisins, sugar, soda, cinnamon and buttermilk, stirring just until moistened. Add 1½ cups of the optional ingredients, any combination. Spoon batter into greased muffin tins, filling ¾ full. Bake 18-20 minutes. Batter may be kept, covered, in the refrigerator for up to 2 weeks.
Yield: 2-3 dozen muffins.

BROWN SUGAR OATMEAL MUFFINS

1	cup old fashioned oats
1	cup whole wheat flour
½	cup flour
2	teaspoons baking powder
½	teaspoon salt
2	large eggs
¾	cup dark brown sugar, packed
¾	cup milk
¼	cup butter melted, or vegetable oil
1	teaspoon vanilla

Mix oats, flours, baking powder and salt in a large bowl. Whisk eggs and brown sugar in a separate bowl. When smooth, whisk in milk, melted butter and vanilla. Pour over dry ingredients. Fold in with a rubber spatula just until dry ingredients are moistened. Pour batter into oiled muffin cups, filling about ⅔ full. Bake at 400 degrees for 20 minutes.
Makes 12 muffins.

PASTA

ITALIAN PASTA SALAD

2	ounces provolone cheese, cubed
½	cup parsley, chopped
3	ounces sliced pepperoni
1	medium zucchini, sliced
1	medium red pepper, chopped
1	medium green pepper, chopped
14	ripe olives
½	red onion, chopped
1	tomato, seeded and chopped
8	ounces spiral pasta, cooked and cooled

VINAIGRETTE:

1	large clove garlic, minced
¼	cup vegetable oil
2	tablespoons olive oil
2	tablespoons balsamic vinegar
1	teaspoon fresh basil or 2 tablespoons dried
½	teaspoon salt
¼	teaspoon oregano
	Freshly ground black pepper to taste

Toss all the salad ingredients together in a large bowl. To make the vinaigrette, whisk the ingredients together or shake in a jar. Pour dressing over salad and toss again. Serve at room temperature.
8-10 servings.

PARTY TORTELLINI SALAD

2	pounds tortellini, 1 pound green, 1 pound white
1	pound Genoa salami, cubed
1	pound provolone cheese, cubed
1½	cups black olives, sliced
1	small red onion, chopped
2	teaspoons seasoned salt, or to taste
2	small peppers, red or green, julienned
1	bottle Italian salad dressing

In separate pans cook the green and white tortellini; drain. Mix tortellini with salami, cheese, olives, onion, peppers and salt. Pour on dressing as needed and toss to blend.
8-10 servings.

BROCCOLI FETTUCCINE SALAD

1	bunch broccoli, cut into bite-sized pieces
1	small red onion, chopped
1	cup Cheddar cheese, shredded
½	pound bacon, fried and crumbled
3	ounces fettuccine, cooked and drained

DRESSING:

½	cup mayonnaise
¼	cup sugar
1	tablespoon vinegar

Mix broccoli, onion, cheese, bacon and pasta in a bowl. Whisk dressing ingredients together and toss over salad.
6-8 servings.

TUNA PASTA SALAD

6	tablespoons olive oil
2	cloves garlic, minced
2	ounces pine nuts
1	cup fresh tomatoes, peeled, seeded and coarsely chopped
1	pound fettuccine, preferably fresh
1	cup white tuna, chunked
½	red pepper, julienned
6	black olives, coarsely chopped
1	tablespoon parsley, chopped
2	tablespoons red wine vinegar
Salt and pepper to taste	

Heat olive oil in a deep skillet and sauté the garlic and pine nuts until the pine nuts are golden. Add the tomatoes and cook briefly. Turn mixture into a large bowl and cool. Cook the fettuccine al dente and drain. Toss pasta with the oil, garlic and pine nuts. Add the remaining ingredients and toss again. Serve at room temperature, garnished with additional parsley.
4 servings.

ROTELLE SALAD

1	pound rotelle pasta, cooked al dente and drained
½	cup sun dried tomatoes, chopped
¼	cup red onion, chopped
1	cup Kalamata olives, pitted
3	cups spinach, sliced thin
¾	pound feta cheese

DRESSING:

½	cup olive oil
3	tablespoons red wine vinegar
1	clove garlic, minced
½	teaspoon salt

Freshly ground pepper to taste

Put cooled pasta in a large bowl. Add tomatoes, onion, olives and spinach. Crumble cheese over the top. Whisk together dressing ingredients and toss with the salad. Serve at room temperature.
8 servings.

BEEF AND PASTA SALAD

1	cup any shape short pasta, cooked
½	cup green onions, sliced
1	tablespoon cider vinegar
1	tablespoon olive oil or vegetable oil
¼	cup mayonnaise
½	teaspoon sugar
1	teaspoon horseradish, grated
1	tablespoon mustard
2	cups bite-sized cold roast beef
1	cup celery, chopped
1	cup broccoli flowerettes
½	cup walnuts, chopped
Salt and pepper to taste	

Mix together the pasta, onion, cider vinegar and oil. Allow to stand 1 hour. Mix together the mayonnaise, sugar, horseradish and mustard. Blend this into the pasta mixture. Toss with the beef, celery and broccoli. Blend thoroughly. Top with walnuts.
Serves 6.

SHRIMP FETTUCCINE

5	green onions, chopped
2	cups mushrooms, sliced
2	cloves garlic, minced
½	cup butter, divided
2	tablespoons olive oil
1	pound raw shrimp, peeled and deveined
Salt and pepper to taste	
8	ounces fettuccine
¾	cup Romano cheese, grated
¾	cup Parmesan cheese, grated
1	cup heavy cream
¼	cup parsley, chopped

In a large skillet sauté the green onions, mushrooms and garlic in ¼ cup butter and 2 tablespoons olive oil. Add shrimp and sauté until pink. Pour off excess liquid; season with salt and pepper. Cover and keep warm. Cook pasta al dente in boiling salted water; drain. In a saucepan melt the remaining 4 tablespoons of butter. Add the pasta, cheeses and cream, mixing well. Combine sauce with the shrimp mixture. Sprinkle with parsley and toss well. Serve immediately.
4 servings.

LINGUINE WITH CLAM SAUCE

1	large onion, chopped
3	cloves garlic, minced
2	cups sliced fresh mushrooms
¼	cup butter or margarine
¼	cup olive oil
1	cup chopped parsley
¼	teaspoon dried oregano
¼	cup dry white wine
2	6½-ounce cans clams, undrained
Salt and pepper to taste	
8	ounces linguine, cooked al dente and drained
¼	cup freshly grated Romano cheese

In a large skillet sauté the onion, garlic and mushrooms in butter and oil until tender. Stir in the parsley, oregano, wine, clams, salt and pepper and heat gently until flavors are blended, 3-5 minutes. Correct seasonings. Toss the sauce with the linguine and serve with grated Romano.
2-3 servings.

SEACOAST SHRIMP AND CRAB LINGUINE

3	tablespoons butter
3	tablespoons shallots, chopped
1	cup fresh mushrooms, sliced
½	pound uncooked shrimp, peeled
1	6-ounce can crab, drained
½	cup Madeira
¼	teaspoon tarragon
1	tablespoon lemon juice
2	teaspoons tomato paste
2	egg yolks
1	cup whipping cream
Salt and pepper to taste	
8	ounces linguine, cooked
Chopped parsley for garnish	

Melt butter in a saucepan. Sauté shallots until soft. Add mushrooms. Sauté until liquid evaporates. Add shrimp and cook until they turn pink. Add crab. Stir in Madeira and cook until reduced by half. Stir in tarragon, lemon juice and tomato paste and mix thoroughly. Combine egg yolks and cream in a separate bowl. Add some of the hot pan juices to the egg yolk/cream mixture; blend. Return mixture very slowly to the saucepan, stirring constantly. Heat through. Do not boil. Serve over cooked linguine. Garnish with chopped parsley. Serves 2.

HAY AND STRAW

9	ounces fettuccine or egg noodles
9	ounces spinach fettuccine
1	pound mushrooms, sliced
4-5	tablespoons butter
1	clove garlic, sliced
Salt to taste	
½	pound sweet Italian sausage
1	cup half and half
¾	cup Parmesan cheese, grated

In a large skillet heat butter and sauté garlic until brown; discard garlic. Add mushrooms and sprinkle with salt. Sauté until lightly browned, 10 minutes. In a separate pan crumble sausage and cook until no longer pink; drain. Combine sausage with mushrooms and keep warm. Warm half and half in the top of a double boiler.

Bring 2 large saucepans of water to a boil and cook pastas separately until tender. Drain and turn into a large heated serving dish. Add sausage and mushroom mixture, Parmesan and half and half and toss gently until well combined. Serve immediately.
6 servings.

FETTUCINE WITH HAM, ZUCCHINI AND SWEET PEPPERS

1	pound lean ham, cut into strips
1	tablespoon olive oil
2	small zucchini, cut into strips
1½	cups sweet pepper strips, any combination of green, red, yellow, orange
1	teaspoon dried oregano
1	clove garlic, pressed
12	ounces fettuccine, fresh or dried
⅔	cup half and half
⅓	cup fresh basil, cut into strips, optional
⅓	cup sun-dried tomatoes, oil packed, optional
2	tablespoons Parmesan cheese, grated

Trim any fat from the ham and set aside. Heat oil in a large skillet over medium high heat. Stir in zucchini, peppers, oregano and garlic; cook until zucchini is tender. Add ham. Cook pasta al dente. Drain and return to the hot pan. Stir in zucchini mixture, cream, basil and tomatoes, if used. Toss until well combined. Sprinkle with Parmesan cheese.
4 servings.

COLETTE'S LINGUINE WITH PESTO SAUCE

2	cloves garlic
2	cups fresh basil leaves
1	cup Italian parsley
12	almonds
12	walnuts
1	tablespoon pine nuts, toasted
3	tablespoons butter, room temperature
½	cup olive oil
½	cup Asiago cheese, grated
½	cup Romano cheese, grated
16	ounces linguine, cooked al dente

In a food processor fitted with a metal blade, drop the garlic down the feed tube and process briefly, 30 seconds. Add the basil, parsley, almonds, walnuts, pine nuts and butter. While processor is running, pour the olive oil down the feed tube in a steady stream and process until smooth. Scrape mixture into a large bowl and combine with Asiago and Romano cheeses. Serve sauce over linguine. 8 servings.

VEGETABLE STROGANOFF

1½ cups fresh cauliflower
flowerettes

1½ cups fresh broccoli
flowerettes

1½ cups thinly sliced carrots

3 cups sliced fresh mushrooms

1 small onion, chopped

1 clove garlic, minced

3 tablespoons butter or
margarine

2 tablespoons all-purpose flour

2 cups milk

½ teaspoon instant chicken
bouillon granules

⅓ cup sliced pitted ripe olives
(optional)

1 cup ricotta cheese

¾ cup sour cream

½ cup Parmesan cheese, grated

1 pound linguine, cooked

Cook cauliflower, broccoli and carrots, covered, in boiling water 5 minutes; drain. Set vegetables aside. Sauté mushrooms, onions, and garlic in butter or margarine for 5 minutes. Stir in flour. Add milk and chicken bouillon granules. Cook and stir until bubbly. Carefully add the vegetables and olives. Stir to blend. Combine ricotta, sour cream and half of the Parmesan cheese. Stir gently into vegetables and heat through. Do not boil. Serve on linguine. Sprinkle with remaining cheese. Serves 6.

SUNDAY NIGHT NOODLES

4	tablespoons butter, divided
½	medium onion, chopped
1	6-ounce can tomato paste
½	tablespoon sugar
Salt and pepper to taste	
¼	teaspoon ground nutmeg
1	10½-ounce can beef consommé
½	pound mushrooms, sliced
2	cups cooked, cubed ham, chicken or a combination of both
2	tablespoons parsley, chopped
Parmesan cheese for garnish	
10	ounces egg noodles, cooked and drained

Melt 2 tablespoons of butter in a saucepan over medium heat. Add onion and cook until soft, 5 minutes. Mix in tomato paste, sugar, salt, pepper, nutmeg and consommé and cook gently, stirring occasionally for 20 minutes. Meanwhile, melt the remaining 2 tablespoons of butter in a skillet and sauté the mushrooms until lightly browned. Add mushrooms to the sauce, along with the meat and parsley. Combine the sauce with the cooked noodles and turn into a buttered 2 quart casserole. Bake in a 350 degree oven for 30-40 minutes. Serve with grated Parmesan cheese.
4-5 servings.

SPAGHETTI WITH SHIITAKE AND TOMATO CREAM SAUCE

4	tablespoons butter
1	pound fresh shiitake mushrooms, stemmed and sliced
1	14-ounce can Italian plum tomatoes, undrained, crushed
1	cup chicken stock
1½	cups heavy cream
½	cup freshly grated Parmesan cheese
8	ounces spaghetti

In a large skillet melt butter over medium heat. Add mushrooms and cook, stirring, until softened, 5 minutes. Add tomatoes, stock and cream. Bring to a boil, stirring constantly. Reduce heat and cook, stirring occasionally, until mixture is reduced by ⅓, 15-20 minutes. Remove from heat and stir in Parmesan cheese. While the sauce is cooking, cook the spaghetti al dente; drain. Before serving, toss the spaghetti with the sauce and garnish with additional Parmesan. 4 servings.

See photo illustration.

PASTA PRIMAVERA

½	cup unsalted butter
1	medium onion, minced
1	clove garlic, pressed
1	pound asparagus, cut diagonally
½	pound mushrooms, sliced
6	ounces cauliflowerets
1	medium zucchini, sliced in rounds
1	carrot, sliced diagonally
1	cup whipping cream
½	cup chicken stock
2	tablespoons fresh basil, or 2 teaspoons dried
1	cup small frozen peas, thawed
2	ounces prosciutto, chopped
5	green onions, chopped
Salt and freshly ground pepper	
1	pound fettuccine or linguine, cooked al dente and drained
1	cup freshly grated Parmesan cheese

Heat a wok or deep skillet over medium high heat. Add butter, onion and garlic and sauté until onion is softened. Mix in asparagus, mushrooms, cauliflower, zucchini and carrots and stir-fry 2 minutes, or until vegetables are crisp-tender. Increase heat to high. Add cream, chicken stock and basil and allow mixture to boil until slightly reduced, 2-3 minutes. Reduce heat and stir in peas, prosciutto and green onion. Cook 1-2 minutes more. Season to taste with salt and pepper. Add cooked pasta to sauce, along with the Parmesan, tossing until well combined.
4-6 servings.

TAGLIATELLE AL BATTIBECCO

3	ounces pancetta, or smoked bacon, cut into ½" cubes
1	14-ounce can tomatoes, undrained, crushed
½	cup butter
3	tablespoons brandy
1½	cups heavy cream
1	cup zucchini, green outer part only, cut into strips
8	ounces pasta, preferably fresh
⅓	cup freshly grated Asiago or Parmesan cheese

Lightly brown pancetta or bacon in a large skillet; add undrained tomatoes. Cook until liquid has been reduced by half. Add the butter, brandy, and cream and cook over medium high heat for about 3 minutes until the mixture just begins to thicken. Blanch the zucchini until just tender; add to the sauce and set aside.

In a large pot of boiling salted water, cook the pasta until half done. Drain and add to the sauce. Toss well and cook over medium heat until the pasta is done. Stir in the cheese and serve immediately. 8 first course servings.

CHICKEN STUFFED SHELLS

½	pound mushrooms, sliced
2	tablespoons butter or margarine
3	cups cooked chicken, cubed
2	tablespoons parsley
1½	teaspoons marjoram
¼	teaspoon nutmeg

Salt and white pepper to taste

½	cup grated Parmesan cheese
1	egg
1½	tablespoons lemon juice
½	cup dry bread crumbs

8-10 ounces jumbo pasta shells

4	ounces Swiss cheese, shredded

3-4 cups spaghetti sauce

Sauté the mushrooms in the butter; set aside. Place the chicken in a food processor fitted with a metal blade and process briefly, 10-15 seconds. Add mushrooms, seasonings, Parmesan, egg and lemon juice and process until chicken is finely chopped and mixture is beginning to look like a paste, 30-40 seconds. Turn into a bowl and mix in bread crumbs.

Cook shells according to package directions; rinse and drain. Put a layer of spaghetti sauce in the bottom of a 9" x 13" baking dish. Spoon filling into shells and place them on top of the sauce. Sprinkle Swiss cheese over the shells and top with the remaining sauce. Bake uncovered in a 350 degree oven for 30 minutes or until hot and bubbly. 4-6 servings.

LAZY LASAGNE

1	pound ground beef or ground turkey
1	14-ounce can tomatoes, undrained
1	6-ounce can tomato paste
1	teaspoon salt, or to taste
1½	teaspoons dried basil
½	teaspoon dried oregano
⅛	teaspoon garlic powder
½	cup water
2	cups ricotta or cottage cheese, drained
¼	cup Parmesan cheese, grated
1	egg, lightly beaten
1	tablespoon parsley flakes
6-8	ounces lasagne noodles, uncooked
2	cups mozzarella cheese, shredded

Cook the ground meat and drain; set aside. Stir together the tomatoes, tomato paste, salt, basil, oregano, garlic powder and water. Cook on the stovetop or in the microwave until mixture boils. Stir in the ground meat. In a separate bowl combine the ricotta, Parmesan, egg and parsley, mixing well. Pour a thin layer of sauce in the bottom of a 9" x 13" glass baking dish. Place a layer of uncooked lasagne noodles over the sauce. Spread ½ of the ricotta mixture over the noodles, followed by ½ the mozzarella. Spoon on ½ of the remaining sauce. Repeat layers, ending with sauce. Cover tightly with plastic wrap. Microwave on high for 15 minutes, rotating once halfway through. Microwave on 50% power for 15-20 minutes, rotating once. Remove plastic wrap and sprinkle with additional Parmesan. Microwave, uncovered, 2 minutes. Let stand 5 minutes. Microwave 5 minutes. Let stand 5 minutes before serving.
8 servings.

WHITE LASAGNE

6	tablespoons butter, divided
½	pound mushrooms, sliced
½	cup dry white wine or vermouth
½	teaspoon dried tarragon
4	tablespoons flour
Salt to taste	
¼	teaspoon nutmeg
¼	teaspoon white pepper
2	cups half and half
2	cups chicken broth
8	ounces lasagne noodles
5	cups cooked chicken breast meat, shredded
12	ounces Swiss cheese, shredded

In a large skillet melt 2 tablespoons of butter and sauté mushrooms until lightly browned. Add wine and tarragon and cook over medium heat until juices have evaporated. Set aside. In a small saucepan melt remaining 4 tablespoons of butter. Whisk in flour, salt, nutmeg and white pepper. Cook 1-2 minutes, stirring. Remove from heat and slowly add half and half and broth. Return to medium heat and cook, stirring, until thickened. Add mushrooms; set aside.

Cook lasagne noodles in boiling water. Rinse with cold water and drain well. Put a thin layer of sauce in the bottom of a greased 9" x 13" baking pan. Top with a layer of noodles. Spread ⅓ of the chicken over the noodles, followed by ⅓ of the sauce and ⅓ of the cheese. Repeat two more times, ending with cheese. Bake uncovered in a 350 degree oven for 40-50 minutes. Let stand 5 minutes before cutting. 8 servings.

RISOTTO WITH BLUE CHEESE AND ARTICHOKES

2	tablespoons olive oil
1	cup onion, finely chopped
1	tablespoon shallots, finely chopped
1	cup Arborio rice
4-5	cups chicken stock, simmering
2	ounces good quality blue cheese, crumbled
1	14-ounce can artichoke hearts, drained and quartered

Salt and freshly ground pepper to taste

In a large saucepan over medium heat, sauté onion and shallots in olive oil until soft. Add rice and stir until rice is coated with oil. Stirring constantly, add 1 cup of the warm chicken stock to the rice. When the liquid has been absorbed, add more stock, ½ cup at a time, cooking gently. Continue to stir and add liquid in small amounts only when the previous liquid has been absorbed. This process should take 25-30 minutes. When rice is tender, remove from heat and add the blue cheese and artichoke hearts, stirring to melt cheese. Serve immediately. 4-5 servings.

WILD RICE CASSEROLE

1	cup wild rice, washed and soaked overnight
1	cup Cheddar cheese, shredded
1	cup chopped ripe olives
1	cup canned tomatoes, undrained
1	cup fresh mushrooms, sliced
½	cup chopped onion
½	cup vegetable oil

Salt and pepper to taste

1	cup hot water

Drain the soaked wild rice. Mix all the ingredients except the water in an ungreased 2½ quart casserole, reserving a small amount of the cheese for garnish. When ready to bake, stir in the hot water. Bake in a 350 degree oven for 1 hour. Sprinkle with the reserved cheese. 6-8 servings.

THANKSGIVING WILD RICE

2	cups wild rice, rinsed and cooked according to package directions
6	strips bacon, cooked crisp and crumbled
1	pound pork sausage, cooked and drained
2	tablespoons butter
1¼	cups diced celery
½	cup chopped onion
½	cup green or red pepper, chopped
1	cup sliced mushrooms
1	2-ounce jar pimento
1	cup half and half
2	cups chicken broth
¾-1	cup cracker crumbs
½	cup chopped pecans
2	eggs, beaten
1½	teaspoons salt
¼	teaspoon ground bay leaf
1	tablespoon parsley flakes
¼	teaspoon black pepper
½	teaspoon dried thyme
1	teaspoon poultry seasoning
¼	cup dry sherry

Mix cooked rice, bacon and sausage together in a large bowl; set aside. In a large skillet melt the butter and sauté the celery, onion, pepper, mushrooms and pimento. Remove from heat and mix in half and half, broth, crumbs, pecans and eggs. Stir in the seasonings and sherry. Combine with rice mixture. Turn into a large casserole and bake in a 350 degree oven for 45-50 minutes. Add a small amount of broth while cooking if mixture seems too dry.
10-12 servings.

SKILLET RICE AND NOODLES

1	bunch green onions
4	tablespoons butter
1	cup long grain rice
1	cup fine egg noodles
3	chicken bouillon cubes
2½	cups boiling water
2	teaspoons bottled steak sauce
½	teaspoon coarsely ground pepper

Wash and trim green onions. Cut white part into ¼″ pieces, measure ⅓ cup and set aside. Cut green part into ¼″ pieces, measure ¼ cup and set aside. In a large skillet melt butter. Add the white part of the onions, the rice and noodles. Cook, stirring constantly, until golden brown, 6 minutes. Dissolve the bouillon cubes in the boiling water and add to the rice mixture. Stir in the steak sauce and pepper. Reduce heat, cover, and cook until the liquid is absorbed and the rice is tender, 20 minutes. Stir in the reserved onion tops before serving. 6 servings.

MEXICAN RICE

¼	cup margarine
1	cup chopped onion
4	cups cooked rice
2	cups sour cream
1	cup cottage cheese
1	large bay leaf, crumbled
½	teaspoon salt
½	teaspoon pepper
¼	teaspoon ground cumin
¼	teaspoon garlic powder
1	4-ounce can chopped green chilies
2	cups Cheddar cheese, shredded

Grease a 2 quart casserole. In a small skillet sauté the onion in margarine; set aside. In a large bowl combine the rice, sour cream, cottage cheese, bay leaf, salt, pepper, cumin and garlic powder. Add the onions and mix well. Layer ½ of the rice mixture in the prepared casserole. Top with half the chopped chilies and half the cheese. Repeat. Bake uncovered in a 375 degree oven for 25 minutes. 10-12 servings.

PARMESAN RICE

1½	tablespoons butter
1	medium onion, chopped
2	cloves garlic, minced
1	cup double-strength chicken broth, canned or homemade
¾	cup long grain rice
½	cup dry white wine
½	cup Parmesan cheese

Melt the butter in a saucepan over medium heat. Add the onion and garlic and cook until softened. Stir in the broth, rice, and wine. Bring to a boil; reduce heat and cook, covered, until the liquid is absorbed, 25-30 minutes. Mix in the Parmesan cheese until melted. 3-4 servings.

TUNA RICE SALAD

3-4 cups cooked rice

1   12½ ounce can tuna

Mayonnaise to moisten

1   medium onion, chopped

1   medium tomato cut in small
    pieces or cherry tomatoes cut
    in half

1 or 2 teaspoons basil

½   teaspoon lemon pepper

Salt to taste

1   tablespoon capers

Cool rice, drain and flake tuna; mix
in remaining ingredients except
capers. Best made 12-24 hours
ahead. Mix capers in just before
serving.
Serves 4-6.

FISH & SEAFOOD

RIDGEWAY SALMON

1	pound snow peas, strings removed
8	ounces linguine
1½	pounds salmon fillet, cut into 4 pieces, skin on
Fresh sorrel or sage leaves	

MARINADE:

¼	cup olive oil
1	tablespoon fresh thyme or ½ teaspoon dried
1	tablespoon fresh marjoram or ½ teaspoon dried
½	teaspoon red pepper flakes
½	cup white wine
Juice of 1 lemon	
4	tablespoons butter, melted
Fresh parsley, snipped	

Prepare marinade by mixing olive oil, herbs, wine and lemon juice in a glass dish. Place salmon in dish and turn to coat on both sides. Cover and let stand 15-30 minutes at room temperature. In the meantime prepare grill for cooking. Coat a mesh grill with olive oil and cover it with sorrel or sage leaves. Place the fish on the herbs skin side down, reserving the marinade. Grill 5-7 minutes, turn and grill until fish flakes. Do not overcook.

While fish cooks, cook linguine according to package directions. Blanch snow peas in boiling water 2-3 minutes; drain and set aside. Place marinade in a saucepan and whisk in 4 tablespoons melted butter. Toss linguine with warmed marinade. To serve, place fish on top of linguine, place snow peas along side and garnish with parsley and lemon slices.

GRILLED SALMON WITH BOURBON

4   **salmon steaks or fillets**

½   **teaspoon salt**

½   **teaspoon garlic salt**

MARINADE:

⅓   **cup soy sauce**

⅓   **cup vegetable oil**

⅓   **cup bourbon**

Sprinkle salmon with salt and garlic salt. Place in a heavy self-sealing plastic storage bag. Mix together the ingredients for the marinade. Pour over the salmon and seal the bag. Marinate for 30 minutes, turning after 15 minutes to coat both sides.

Prepare the grill. When coals are white, place salmon on grill, 5″ - 6″ above coals. Grill for 7-8 minutes. Turn over and grill for an additional 7-8 minutes. Baste with marinade while salmon cooks. Fish will flake when done. Do not overcook. 4 servings.

FISH & SEAFOOD

GRILLED MARINATED SALMON

6-8 salmon steaks, about 5 pounds

1 tablespoon kosher salt or rock salt

MARINADE:

⅓ cup olive oil

3 large cloves garlic, minced

3 tablespoons fresh lemon juice

1 tablespoon dried parsley, or 3 tablespoons fresh

1 teaspoon dried dillweed, or 1 tablespoon fresh

1 teaspoon dried rosemary, or 1 tablespoon fresh

1 teaspoon dried basil, or 1 tablespoon fresh

½ fresh lemon, thinly sliced

Gently rub salt on both sides of the salmon and place skin side down in a shallow glass dish. Mix together the marinade ingredients and pour over the salmon. Marinate for 2 hours at room temperature, or overnight in the refrigerator.

When ready to cook, prepare grill. When coals are hot, grill skin side down for 7-9 minutes. Turn over and grill 4-5 minutes. Fish will flake when done; do not overcook. 6-8 servings.

PESCADO BORRACHO (DRUNKEN FISH)

1	3-pound dressed fish or 2 pounds fillets
½	teaspoon crushed red pepper
⅓	cup dry red wine
½	cup chopped onion
1	clove garlic, minced
2	tablespoons olive oil
3	medium tomatoes, peeled, seeded and chopped
⅓	cup water
¼	cup parsley, snipped
1	teaspoon sugar
½	teaspoon salt
½	teaspoon oregano
¼	teaspoon cumin
½	cup pimento-stuffed olives, sliced
1	tablespoon capers

In a medium saucepan, cook onion and garlic in olive oil until translucent. Add red pepper to pan along with wine, tomatoes, water, parsley, sugar, salt, oregano and cumin. Bring to a boil; reduce heat and simmer, covered, for 5 minutes. Place fish in a greased 9″ x 13″ baking dish. Season the cavity of the fish with salt and pepper. Stir sliced olives and capers into the sauce and pour over the fish. Cover and bake in a 350 degree oven for 40-60 minutes or until fish flakes easily.
6-8 servings.

FISH & SEAFOOD

HUNGARIAN SNAPPER

2	pounds red snapper fillets, ¾" thick
2	leeks, white part only, chopped
1	teaspoon vegetable oil
1	green pepper, julienned
1	red pepper, julienned
1	yellow pepper, julienned
1	tablespoon paprika
1	tablespoon tomato purée
1	cup champagne or dry white wine
½	cup clam juice
¾	cup sour cream
¼	cup heavy cream

Sauté leeks in oil. Add peppers and sauté for 2 minutes. Remove from heat and set aside. In another pan poach the fish pieces in the wine and clam juice until opaque. Remove fish from liquid and keep warm, covered. Reduce poaching liquid to ½ cup. Add leeks and peppers, tomato purée and paprika. Blend heavy cream with sour cream and add to sauce. Heat through, but do not allow to boil. Add fish and warm gently. Serve with boiled new potatoes or buttered noodles.
6 servings.

CHAMPAGNE SOLE

2	**oranges, sliced**
2	**pounds sole fillets**

Olive oil

1	**sprig fresh tarragon per fillet, or 1½ teaspoons dried**

CHAMPAGNE SAUCE:

2	**tablespoons butter**
1	**tablespoon flour**
1	**cup champagne, or dry white wine**
1	**cup heavy cream**
½	**teaspoon tarragon**

Oil grill and place orange slices on oiled surface. Brush sole with olive oil and place on orange slices. Cover the sole with the tarragon. Grill until sole is opaque; do not turn. Cooking time should be about 10 minutes.

For the sauce, melt butter in a saucepan. Whisk in flour; cook, stirring, 1 minute. Stir in champagne and cook over medium heat until reduced by one half. Stir in cream and tarragon and cook gently until sauce thickens. Serve sauce over cooked fish. 4 servings.

BAKED FISH LOUISIANA

4	6-ounce fish steaks such as red snapper, halibut or swordfish, ¾″ - 1″ thick
2	tablespoons olive oil
4	green peppers, julienned
1	teaspoon fresh lemon juice
3	medium onions, chopped
4	cloves garlic, minced
2	cups tomatoes, with juice
1	teaspoon oregano
1	tablespoon chili powder, or to taste
2	tablespoons cilantro
2	tablespoons parsley, chopped
1-2	tablespoons butter

Sauté the pepper strips in 1 tablespoon olive oil, seasoning with salt and pepper. Add lemon juice; set aside. In another pan sauté the onion and garlic in 1 tablespoon olive oil. Add the tomatoes, oregano, chili powder, cilantro and parsley. Simmer for 25 minutes. Place the fish in an oiled baking dish. Dot with butter and bake in a 425 degree oven for 20 minutes or until done. Pour the sauce over the fish. Top with the green peppers and return to the oven for 3-5 minutes to heat through and blend flavors. Serve with rice.
4 servings.

SHRIMP CREOLE

½ cup onion, chopped

½ cup celery, chopped

½ cup green pepper, chopped

1 clove garlic, minced

2 tablespoons vegetable oil

2 cups canned tomatoes, undrained

1 8-ounce can seasoned tomato sauce

1½ teaspoons salt

1 teaspoon sugar

1 teaspoon chili powder

1 tablespoon Worcestershire sauce

Dash red pepper sauce

1 teaspoon cornstarch

2 tablespoons water

2 pounds raw shrimp, shelled

Cook onion, celery, green pepper and garlic in hot oil until tender. Add tomatoes, tomato sauce and seasonings. Simmer uncovered for 45 minutes. Mix cornstarch with water and stir into sauce. Cook, stirring, until thickened. Add shrimp and simmer 5 minutes or until shrimp are done. Serve over rice.

4 servings.

FISH & SEAFOOD

SHRIMP SINCLAIR

3	pounds shrimp, cooked and cleaned
½	pound fresh mushrooms, sliced
2	tablespoons unsalted butter
3	cups cooked long grain rice (1½ cups uncooked)
3	cups sharp Cheddar cheese, shredded
½	cup heavy cream
3	tablespoons ketchup
1	tablespoon fresh lemon juice
3	tablespoons white Worcestershire sauce
Salt and white pepper to taste	
1	clove garlic, minced

Sauté mushrooms in unsalted butter. Mix cream, ketchup, lemon juice, Worcestershire sauce, salt, pepper and garlic. In 3 quart casserole, combine shrimp, cheese, rice and sautéed mushrooms; gently mix with cream sauce. May refrigerate before baking. Bake 350 degrees 25-35 minutes. Serves 6.

EASY SHRIMP STEW

2	pounds raw shrimp in the shell
1 - 1½ pounds smoked sausage, cut in 2" pieces	
4-6 ears corn	
1	stalk celery
⅛	cup salt
1	tablespoon shrimp boil spices

Bring 1 gallon of water to a boil in a large stock pot. Add celery, salt and spices. Add sausages and boil 7 minutes. Add corn and boil 7 minutes. Add shrimp: reduce heat and cook 4 minutes or until shrimp are pink. Drain and serve all together in a large bowl. Pass melted butter. 4 servings.

BUTTERY SHRIMP DUNK

4	tablespoons butter, melted
4	tablespoons margarine, melted
⅛	cup Worcestershire sauce
1	tablespoon black pepper, or to taste
¼	teaspoon rosemary, crushed
½	teaspoon hot pepper sauce
½	teaspoon salt
2	cloves garlic, minced
2	lemons, 1 sliced, 1 juiced
1½	pounds raw shrimp, shelled and deveined

Preheat oven to 400 degrees. In a bowl mix all the ingredients except for the lemon slices and shrimp. Pour ½ cup of this sauce in a baking dish. Layer the shrimp and lemon slices in the dish and pour remaining sauce over. Bake 15-20 minutes, stirring once. Serve from baking dish and pass French bread for dipping.
2-3 servings.

SCALLOPED SCALLOPS

1½	pounds scallops
½	cup butter
4	green onions, chopped
1	teaspoon dried thyme
3	dashes hot pepper sauce
1	tablespoon white Worcestershire sauce
3	tablespoons parsley, chopped
1½	cups saltine crackers
¼	cup half and half
¼	cup dry vermouth, or fish bouillon
Paprika	

Wash and drain the scallops; set aside. In a skillet melt the butter and sauté the green onions until soft. Stir in the thyme, hot pepper sauce, Worcestershire and parsley. Add the cracker crumbs and toss until coated with butter. Put ⅓ of the cracker crumbs in the bottom of a 1½ quart baking dish. Top with ½ of the scallops. Repeat layers, ending with a layer of crumbs. Mix the half and half with the vermouth or bouillon and pour over the top. Dust with paprika. Bake in a 350 degree oven for 35 minutes or until lightly browned.
4 servings.

CRAB MORNAY

1	avocado
1	tablespoon lemon juice
4	tablespoons butter
¼	pound fresh mushrooms, sliced
12	ounces crabmeat, preferably Dungeness
1	cup mornay sauce
¼	cup sherry
¼	cup white wine
2	egg yolks
4	cherry tomatoes
½	cup grated Parmesan cheese
2	lemons, thinly sliced

MORNAY SAUCE:

2	cups half and half
4	tablespoons butter
4	tablespoons flour
3	ounces crabmeat juice or fish bouillon
3	ounces Cheddar cheese, shredded

Salt and pepper to taste

To make the sauce, melt 4 tablespoons of butter in a saucepan, add flour and stir until butter is absorbed. Add the half and half slowly, stirring constantly. Add the crabmeat juice or bouillon and cook over low heat for 10 minutes. Add the cheese and cook over low heat for an additional 10 minutes, stirring frequently. Season to taste.

After preparing sauce, peel and cut the avocado into 8 pieces; brush with lemon juice to prevent discoloration. Melt butter in a saucepan and sauté mushrooms briefly. Add crabmeat and cook for 3 minutes. Stir in 1 cup of mornay sauce, sherry and white wine; simmer for 15 minutes. Remove pan from heat and cool slightly. Add egg yolks, stirring. Arrange crabmeat in 4 individual ramekins with 2 slices of avocado and 1 cherry tomato, halved, on top of each serving. Sprinkle with Parmesan cheese and bake in a 400 degree oven until browned. Garnish with lemon slices.
4 servings.

CRAB CRUNCH

1	can frozen shrimp soup, thawed
2	tablespoons sherry
1	16-ounce can crab, lump backfin preferred
1	cup celery, chopped
1	small onion, chopped
½	cup mayonnaise
1	tablespoon Worchestershire sauce
1	cup crushed potato chips or seasoned bread crumbs

Mix first 7 ingredients in the order listed. Turn into a greased 8" x 8" pan. Top with potato chips or crumbs. Bake in a preheated 350 degree oven for 45 minutes.
6 servings.

SOUTHERN CRAB CAKES

2	slices of white bread, crusts removed
1	egg, lightly beaten
1	tablespoon mayonnaise
1	teaspoon dry mustard
⅛	teaspoon red pepper
1	teaspoon Worcestershire sauce
1	teaspoon parsley, minced
1	scant tablespoon baking powder
1	pound flaked crabmeat
Butter for oil or frying	

Break bread into small pieces and mix with beaten egg. Add remaining ingredients and mix thoroughly. Shape into patties and refrigerate for 1 hour. Fry in butter or oil.
2-3 servings.

SALMON LOAF WITH CUCUMBER SAUCE

1	cup pink salmon, drained and flaked
1	cup cracker crumbs
⅔	cup milk
2	tablespoons onion, chopped
2	tablespoons butter, melted
2	eggs, beaten
Dash pepper	
1	tablespoon lemon juice

CUCUMBER SAUCE:

½	cup sour cream
½	cup chopped cucumber
½	teaspoon lemon juice
¼	teaspoon dill weed
¼	teaspoon salt

Mix ingredients for salmon loaf together and place in a greased loaf pan. Bake 50 minutes in preheated 375 degree oven. Salmon may be served hot or cold. For the cucumber sauce, mix all ingredients in a blender, chill. Serve over sliced salmon loaf.
Serves 4-6.

SEAFOOD CASSEROLE

4	tablespoons butter, divided
2	cups celery, chopped
½	cup scallions, sliced
1	cup mushrooms, sliced
1	can water chestnuts, sliced
4	hard cooked eggs, chopped
2	cups shrimp, cooked and shelled
1	6½-ounce can crabmeat
2	cups mayonnaise, or "lite" mayonnaise
1	cup crushed potato chips

Sauté celery, scallions and mushrooms in 2 tablespoons butter; set aside. Combine the water chestnuts, eggs, shrimp and crabmeat. Stir in the cooked vegetables and mayonnaise. Place in a 2 quart baking dish, top with the potato chips and dot with the remaining 2 tablespoons butter. Bake in a 350 degree oven for 45 minutes or until bubbly and brown. 6 servings.

PERFECT SCALLOPED OYSTERS

1	pint oysters, liquor reserved
2	cups saltines, coarsely crushed
½	cup butter, melted
½	teaspoon salt
Dash pepper	
¾	cup heavy cream or half and half
¼	teaspoon Worcestershire sauce

After draining oysters, reserve ¼ cup of the oyster liquor. Combine cracker crumbs, butter, salt and pepper. Spread ⅓ of the buttered crumbs in a small casserole. Cover with half the oysters. Spread an additional ⅓ of the crumbs and top with the remaining oysters. Combine cream, reserved liquor, and Worcestershire sauce and pour over the oysters. Cover with the remaining crumbs. Bake in a 350 degree oven for 40 minutes. 4 servings.

LEMONY TUNA

½	cup fresh chopped parsley
1	bunch green onions, sliced
½	cup celery, diced
2	cloves garlic, minced
2	cups fresh mushrooms, sliced
8	tablespoons butter, divided
3	tablespoons flour
¼	teaspoon salt
¼	teaspoon nutmeg
¾	cup heavy cream
1	egg yolk, beaten
1	tablespoon fresh lemon juice
2	6½ ounce cans solid white tuna in water, drained and flaked
1	cup Swiss cheese, shredded

Sauté the first five ingredients in 6 tablespoons butter until lightly browned. For cream sauce, make a roux of 2 tablespoons butter, flour, salt and nutmeg. Add cream, stirring until thickened. Remove from heat; stir in a small amount of sauce into egg yolk. Add egg mixture to sauce, stirring in lemon juice. Stir sauce and sautéed ingredients together; gently fold in tuna. Place in 4 individual ramekins. Top with cheese and broil until cheese is melted. Serve with rice if desired. May be made ahead and baked 20 minutes in 350 degree oven before adding cheese.

MUSTARD SAUCE FOR SEAFOOD

1	cup butter
2	teaspoons Worcestershire sauce
2	teaspoons prepared mustard
2	tablespoons chili sauce
3	dashes hot pepper sauce
4	teaspoons fresh lemon juice
2	teaspoons chopped parsley

Heat all ingredients together until bubbly.

JOE'S STONE CRAB SAUCE

3½	tablespoons dry mustard
1	cup mayonnaise
2	teaspoons Worcestershire sauce
1	teaspoon steak sauce
1	tablespoon whipping cream

Mix all of the ingredients together. Blend thoroughly. Wonderful with stone crab or any other cold seafood.

DILL BUTTER SAUCE

½	cup melted butter
¼	cup finely chopped fresh dill
¼	cup freshly squeezed lemon juice
2	tablespoons tomato paste

Combine all ingredients and stir well to blend. Brush mixture on lobster while it is broiling. Yield: about 1 cup.

POULTRY

POULTRY

MICHIGAN BOUNTY CORNISH HENS

4	Rock Cornish hens, 1½ pounds each
1	cup chicken stock or bouillon
¼	cup wild rice
6	tablespoons butter
2	cups cubed stuffing
½	cup chopped onion
½	cup chopped apple
¼	cup chopped pecans
2	teaspoons dried parsley flakes
¼	teaspoon rubbed sage
¼	teaspoon salt
⅛	teaspoon ground thyme
Dash nutmeg	
1	teaspoon dried savory

Preheat oven to 350 degrees. Rinse hens and pat dry; set aside. In a 2 quart saucepan bring chicken stock to a boil. Stir in rice and 3 tablespoons butter. Simmer, covered, 10 minutes. Remove from heat and stir in stuffing, onion, apples, pecans, parsley, sage, salt, thyme and nutmeg. Stuff each hen with ¾ cup of the mixture. Tie legs together and place breast side up on a rack in a roasting pan. Melt 3 tablespoons butter and blend in savory. Brush on hens. Bake 1-1¼ hours, basting with butter every 20 minutes until meat near bone on underside of hen is no longer pink and juices run clear. Serve with garden vegetables.
4 servings.

See photo illustration.

MEXICAN MEATLOAF

1	pound ground turkey
1	15-ounce can tomato sauce
¼	cup chopped onion
2	tablespoons chopped green pepper
⅓	cup crushed tortilla chips
1	package taco seasoning mix

Mix all ingredients together, reserving 1 cup tomato sauce for topping. Pat into a 9" x 5" x 3" loaf pan. Top with reserved tomato sauce. Bake in a 350 degree oven for 35-40 minutes.
4 servings.

RICH FRUIT POULTRY STUFFING

1   cup prunes

1   cup raisins

Whiskey

1   cup pecans, chopped

1   cup apples, cored and
    chopped

1   cup celery, chopped

1   cup onions, chopped

2   cups bread crumbs or
    croutons

Salt and pepper to taste

1   can chicken broth

Cover prunes and raisins with whiskey and let soak 2 hours. Combine soaked fruit with the other ingredients, using enough chicken broth to moisten. The ingredient amounts may be varied to individual taste. Dressing may be stuffed into a turkey or other fowl or it may be cooked in a casserole. This amount will fill a 12 pound turkey. Double or triple quantities for larger birds.

COURTON (French Canadian Pork Stuffing)

1   pound lean pork, ground
    twice

1   medium onion, chopped

1   tablespoon ground cloves

1   tablespoon ground cinnamon

¼   teaspoon pepper

Salt to taste

2-3 medium potatoes, peeled and
    cubed

Place pork, onions and seasonings in a saucepan and cover with 1-2 cups water. Bring to a boil, reduce heat and simmer, covered, over low heat for 2½-3 hours. Watch liquid during cooking time, adding more only if necessary. Liquid should be completely reduced after 3 hours. In the meantime, boil the potatoes separately until tender. After the pork has cooked, mash in the potatoes. Use as a stuffing for chicken or turkey.

Note: Courton may also be eaten as a side dish. Or, if desired, remove some of the meat mixture before adding potatoes. Chill and use as a spread for crackers or toast.

TURKEY POT PIE

3	tablespoons butter
¾	cup finely chopped onion
½	pound mushrooms, sliced
3	tablespoons all purpose flour
½	teaspoon salt, optional
½	teaspoon dried rosemary
Pepper to taste	
2	chicken bouillon cubes, dissolved in 1¼ cups boiling water
½	cup whipping cream
3	cups cooked turkey, or chicken, cubed
2	tablespoons dry sherry
3	medium potatoes, peeled, cubed and cooked tender
2	medium carrots, peeled, sliced and cooked tender
Pastry for a 9″ pie	

In a saucepan over medium heat, melt butter. Add onion and mushrooms and sauté until onions are transparent. Stir in flour, salt, pepper, and rosemary and cook until bubbly. Remove from heat and stir in bouillon and cream. Return to heat and cook until thickened, stirring constantly. Add sherry, vegetables and turkey. Spoon mixture into a 2½ quart casserole. Roll out pastry to fit over filling. Pinch dough to seal and crimp edges. Cut a slit in the center. Brush with egg yolk wash if desired. Bake in a 425 degree oven for 20-25 minutes or until crust is golden.
6 servings.

HOT CHICKEN SALAD

2	cups cooked chicken, diced
2	cups celery, diced
½	cup sour cream
½	cup mayonnaise
2	tablespoons lemon juice
½	cup mushrooms, sliced
½	cup slivered almonds
1	teaspoon salt
½	cup Cheddar cheese, shredded
½	cup potato chips, crushed

Preheat oven to 425 degrees. Use a nonstick vegetable spray to coat a 2 quart baking dish. Combine all ingredients except potato chips and place in the prepared pan. Top with the chips and bake for 20 minutes. 8 servings.

POULTRY

CAJUN STYLE DRUMSTICKS

8	chicken drumsticks
2	cups buttermilk
¼	cup butter or margarine, melted
½	cup all-purpose flour
½	cup cornmeal
1¼	teaspoons garlic powder
1¼	teaspoons onion powder
1¼	teaspoons chili powder
1¼	teaspoons dried thyme
1¼	teaspoons dried oregano
1¼	teaspoons paprika
1	teaspoon salt
¾	teaspoon ground cumin
¼	teaspoon black pepper
¼	teaspoon white pepper
¼	teaspoon red pepper

Place chicken in shallow baking dish; pour buttermilk over the top. Cover and chill for 8 hours. Combine flour, cornmeal and seasonings in a plastic bag. Drain chicken. Roll in butter and shake 1-2 pieces at a time in the bag until coated. Arrange chicken on a rack in a roasting pan. Drizzle with any remaining butter. Bake in a 400 degree oven for 15 minutes. Turn chicken; reduce heat to 350 degrees and continue to bake for 30-35 minutes, or until done. 4 servings.

CHICKEN WELLINGTON

1   6-ounce box long grain and
    wild rice mix

Grated peel from 1 orange

1   tablespoon fresh parsley,
    chopped

Seasoned salt and pepper to taste

6   chicken breast halves, skinned
    and boned

1   egg white

1   10-ounce package frozen patty
    shells, thawed in refrigerator

3-4 tablespoons milk

SAUCE:

1   12-ounce jar red currant jelly

½   teaspoon Dijon mustard

1   tablespoon orange juice

2   tablespoons white wine

Cook rice according to package
directions. Add orange peel,
parsley, seasoned salt and pepper
to taste. Set aside to cool. Pound
chicken breasts to flatten slightly.
Sprinkle with salt and pepper. Beat
egg white until soft peaks form;
fold into rice mixture.

On a floured pastry cloth roll out
patty shells into 6 8" circles. Put a
chicken breast in the center of each
circle and top with ¼ - ⅓ cup of the
rice mixture. Fold the sides of the
pastry in and then roll up jelly roll
style. Place the pastries in a shallow
baking dish seam side down. Cover
with foil and refrigerate overnight.
Do not remove from refrigerator
until ready to bake. Preheat oven to
375 degrees. Brush pastries with
milk. Bake uncovered for 35-45
minutes. If dough browns too
quickly, cover loosely with foil.
While chicken cooks, make the
sauce. Heat jelly in a small
saucepan. Gradually stir in
mustard, orange juice and wine. To
serve, place pastry on additional
rice, if desired, and serve with
warm sauce.
6 servings.

POULTRY

TERIYAKI CHICKEN SAUTÉ

6	chicken breast halves, skinned and boned
3	tablespoons all purpose flour
	Non-stick vegetable spray
¼	cup butter
⅓	cup teriyaki sauce
3	tablespoons lemon juice
1	teaspoon minced garlic, or garlic powder
½	teaspoon sugar

Dust chicken with flour. Coat a large skillet with vegetable spray. Melt butter over medium high heat, add chicken and brown lightly on both sides, 5-7 minutes. Remove chicken, stir in teriyaki sauce, lemon juice, garlic and sugar. Return chicken to pan. Simmer 3 minutes, turn breasts over and cook 3 minutes more, or until tender. Chicken may be browned and sauce mixed ahead; simmer breasts just before serving. 6 servings.

CHICKEN EVAN

4	chicken breasts, skinned and boned
¼	cup seasoned bread crumbs
3	tablespoons butter, divided
1	clove garlic, minced
1	tablespoon parsley, minced
4-5	fresh mushrooms, sliced
8	oysters, chopped
	Juice from ½ lemon
1	tablespoon Worcestershire sauce
4	artichoke bottoms, quartered
¼	cup white wine
4	thin slices prosciutto

Season chicken with salt and pepper and sprinkle with bread crumbs. Melt 1 tablespoon butter in a skillet and sauté garlic, parsley, and mushrooms for 2 minutes. Add oysters, lemon juice, Worcestershire sauce, artichoke bottoms and wine; simmer 5 minutes.

In a separate pan sauté the chicken breasts in 2 tablespoons butter until brown. Place chicken in a baking dish and cover with the sauce. Top with slices of prosciutto. Bake in a 350 degree oven for 20 minutes or until chicken is tender. 4 servings.

TEXAS PIÑA COLADA CHICKEN

1	16-ounce can sliced pineapple
¼	cup dark rum
¼	cup soy sauce
2	tablespoons cream of coconut
1½	teaspoons grated fresh ginger
1	teaspoon garlic, pressed
¾	teaspoon black pepper
1½	teaspoons cornstarch
·12	chicken thighs

Drain pineapple and reserve juice. Mix juice, rum, soy sauce, cream of coconut, ginger, garlic and pepper. Blend in cornstarch. Arrange chicken in a single layer in a baking dish and pour sauce mixture over. Cover and let stand several hours or overnight in the refrigerator.

Preheat oven to 400 degrees and cook chicken skin side down for 40 minutes. Turn pieces and bake for 20 minutes longer. Top with pineapple slices and bake 5 minutes more.
4-6 servings.

CHICKEN HELENE

1	2½-3 pound chicken, cut up
3-4	tablespoons flour, seasoned with salt and pepper
6	tablespoons butter, divided
1	cup sliced fresh mushrooms
2	tablespoons flour
¾	cup chicken broth
½	cup dry white wine
	Salt and pepper
¼	cup green onions, thinly sliced
1	9-ounce package frozen artichoke hearts, cooked and drained

Dust chicken with seasoned flour. Melt 4 tablespoons of butter in a shallow baking pan. Place chicken in pan, skin side down. Bake, uncovered, in a 350 degree oven for 45 minutes, until almost tender. Melt remaining 2 tablespoons of butter in a saucepan. Sauté mushrooms until tender. Stir in flour and cook briefly. Slowly add broth and wine and cook, stirring constantly, until smooth and thickened. Add salt and pepper to taste. Remove chicken from oven. Turn pieces over and sprinkle with green onions and artichokes. Pour sauce over the top. Return to oven, reduce heat to 325 degrees and bake for 25 minutes longer.
4 servings.

QUICK LEMON CHICKEN

4	whole chicken breasts, skinned, boned and halved
½	cup cornstarch
½	teaspoon salt
⅛	teaspoon pepper
¼	cup water
4	egg yolks, slightly beaten
½	cup vegetable oil
4	green onions, sliced

SAUCE:

1½	cups water
½	cup lemon juice
3	tablespoons light brown sugar, firmly packed
3½	tablespoons honey
3	tablespoons cornstarch
2	teaspoons instant chicken bouillon granules
1	teaspoon ginger root, peeled and grated

Pound chicken breasts with a mallet until slightly flattened. Combine cornstarch, salt and pepper in a small bowl. Gradually blend in water and egg yolks. Pour oil into a wok heated to 375 degrees. Dip chicken pieces into egg mixture and fry 2 or 3 at a time in the hot oil until golden, about 5 minutes. Drain on paper towel and keep warm while cooking remaining chicken.

Combine all sauce ingredients in a small saucepan and stir until blended. Cook, stirring constantly, over medium heat until sauce thickens, 5-7 minutes.

To serve, cut each chicken piece into 3 or 4 pieces and arrange on a plate. Top with green onion slices and sauce.
4-6 servings.

CHICKEN SALTIMBOCCA

6	whole chicken breasts, boned and skinned
4-6	thin slices prosciutto, or boiled ham
6	slices mozzarella
1	medium tomato, seeded and chopped
½	teaspoon dried sage
½	cup dried bread crumbs
4	tablespoons Parmesan cheese, grated
2	tablespoons snipped parsley
4	tablespoons margarine, melted

Place chicken breast on a board, cover with plastic wrap and pound until slightly flattened. Place a slice of prosciutto and a slice of mozzarella on each breast. Top with tomato and sage. Tuck in sides and roll up jelly roll style, pressing to seal. Combine crumbs, Parmesan cheese and parsley. Dip chicken in margarine and then in crumbs. Place in a shallow 9" x 13" baking pan and bake in a 350 degree oven for 45 minutes.
6 servings.

INDIAN CHICKEN CURRY

3-3½ pounds chicken pieces

1　medium onion, chopped

2　cloves garlic, minced

1　1" piece ginger root

2　tablespoons vegetable oil

2　tablespoons butter

1½ cups water

2½ teaspoons tumeric

1¼ teaspoons cumin

1¼ teaspoons mustard seeds

1¼ teaspoons fennel seeds

1　teaspoon crushed red pepper

¾　teaspoon ground coriander

5　cardamom seeds

1　cinnamon stick

¼　teaspoon ground mace, or nutmeg

Salt

Juice of 1 lemon

Rinse chicken and pat dry. Peel ginger root and slice thinly. Heat oil and butter in a large skillet. Add chicken pieces and brown on all sides over high heat. Add onion, garlic, and ginger and stir until onion is translucent. Pour in water and scrape skillet well. Mix in remaining seasonings, except lemon. Cover skillet and simmer over low heat for 3 hours or until chicken is very well cooked. Stir in lemon juice. Serve over steamed rice.

4 servings.

LEMON HERB CHICKEN

4	**whole chicken breasts, skinned, boned and halved**
2	**tablespoons unsalted butter**
2	**tablespoons oil**
6	**tablespoons whipping cream**

Salt and pepper to taste

2	**tablespoons parsley, finely chopped**

MARINADE:

2	**tablespoons finely chopped lemon zest**
¼	**cup lemon juice**
2	**tablespoons oil**
½	**cup dry white wine**
1	**teaspoon honey**
¼	**teaspoon coarsely cracked pepper**
¼	**cup finely chopped herbs, any combination, parsley, thyme, basil, rosemary, oregano, chives**

Combine marinade ingredients in a small bowl. Whisk until blended. In a large, shallow non-metallic dish arrange chicken pieces and pour marinade over. Cover and refrigerate 4 hours. Remove chicken and pat dry, reserving marinade. Melt butter and oil in a large skillet over medium high heat. Add chicken pieces and saute 5-7 minutes on each side until tender and brown. Remove to a platter and keep warm. Drain off excess oil and add reserved marinade to pan. Boil until reduced to ½ cup. Add cream and boil for 3 minutes. Season with salt and pepper to taste. Return chicken to pan and heat through. Serve garnished with parsley and lemon slices.
4 servings.

SESAME CHICKEN

¼	cup soy sauce
1	tablespoon sugar
1	tablespoon dry sherry
½	teaspoon ground ginger
2-3	cloves garlic, pressed
4	whole chicken breasts, skinned, boned and halved
1	egg
⅓	cup flour
⅓	cup sesame seeds
2	tablespoons butter or margarine
2	tablespoons peanut oil

Combine first 5 ingredients in a shallow baking pan, stirring to dissolve sugar. Place chicken in pan and turn to coat with marinade. Cover and refrigerate at least 1 hour. Preheat a 9" x 13" baking pan in a 475 degree oven. Beat the egg with 2 tablespoons of the marinade. Stir together the flour and sesame seeds on a plate. Dip chicken pieces in the egg mixture and then in the flour. When the pan is heated, add the butter and oil. When the butter has melted, add the chicken, turning to coat on both sides. Bake, uncovered, for 5-6 minutes. Carefully turn chicken and cook 4-5 minutes longer, or until chicken is no longer pink inside.
4-6 servings.

ROSEMARY CHICKEN

12	serving pieces of chicken
¼	cup olive oil
	Juice from 3 large lemons
1	teaspoon Worcestershire sauce
3	cloves garlic, minced
½	teaspoon dried rosemary
¼	teaspoon salt
1	teaspoon tamari sauce

Combine olive oil, lemon juice, Worcestershire sauce, garlic, rosemary, salt and tamari sauce; mix well. Place chicken in a glass baking dish and pour mixture over, stirring to coat. Marinate, covered, in the refrigerator overnight. Bake, covered, in a 300 degree oven for 1 hour. Uncover, raise heat to 350 degrees, and bake for 30 minutes longer. Baste chicken occasionally while it cooks.
4-6 servings.

FETA CHICKEN BREASTS

4	whole boneless chicken breasts
¼	cup all purpose flour
¼	cup olive oil
⅛	teaspoon cayenne pepper
½	pound mushrooms, sliced
¼	cup butter
8	slices feta cheese, 1-ounce each

Halve chicken breasts, remove skin and pound between wax paper until thin. Dredge chicken in flour. Heat oil in a large skillet and brown chicken on both sides. Place chicken in a 9" x 13" baking pan and sprinkle with cayenne. Bake in a 375 degree oven for 30 minutes.

While chicken bakes, sauté mushrooms in butter until lightly browned. When chicken is cooked, remove from oven and top with mushrooms. Place a slice of feta cheese on each piece of chicken and broil until cheese is slightly browned.
6-8 servings.

RED SUNSET CHICKEN

1	3-3½ pound chicken, cut into serving pieces
2	tablespoons olive oil
1	medium onion, chopped
1	large tomato, chopped
1	medium green pepper, chopped
1	tablespoon Hungarian paprika
1	teaspoon salt
2-3	tablespoons sour cream, optional

Remove skin from chicken pieces; set chicken aside. Sauté onion in olive oil until soft. Add tomato, green pepper, paprika and salt. Cover and cook over low heat for 15 minutes, or until thickened. Add chicken and a small amount of water, stirring to coat chicken. Simmer, uncovered, until the chicken is cooked, 30-40 minutes. Add sour cream to the sauce if desired, but after adding, do not allow sauce to boil. Serve with buttered noodles.
4 servings.

CHICKEN WITH CUCUMBERS

2	medium cucumbers, unpeeled
2	chicken bouillon cubes, or 2 teaspoons bouillon granules
2	cups water
3	cloves garlic, pressed
4	boneless, skinless chicken breast halves
1	cup plain low-fat yogurt
1½	teaspoons lemon juice
1	tablespoon cornstarch
½	teaspoon dried dillweed

Wash cucumbers, remove ends and score vertically with the tines of a fork. Cut in half lengthwise, remove seeds and cut into ¼" thick slices. Set aside. In a large skillet dissolve bouillon in water; add garlic and bring to a boil. Add chicken and poach gently for 8 minutes, or until no longer pink.

While chicken is cooking, mix yogurt, lemon juice, cornstarch and dillweed; set aside. Add cucumbers to chicken and poach an additional 4 minutes. Remove chicken and cucumbers to a warm serving platter. Discard all but one cup of the poaching liquid. Return the cup of liquid to the skillet. Add the yogurt mixture and cook, stirring constantly, until thickened; do not boil. Pour sauce over chicken and cucumbers and serve garnished with lemon slices.
4 servings.

CHICKEN ENCORE

1	roasting chicken
	Yellow onions
1-2	teaspoons butter or margarine
	Garlic pepper seasoning

Rinse chicken and pat dry. Peel onions and pack into the chicken cavity. Rub butter over chicken. Sprinkle generously with garlic pepper seasoning. Place in a shallow roasting pan and bake in a 350 degree oven for one hour or until tender and cooked through.
3-4 servings.

ARIZONA CHICKEN

6 chicken breast halves, skinned

Salt to taste

¼ cup plus 1 tablespoon
vegetable oil

1 cup uncooked long grain rice

1 clove garlic, pressed

1 12-ounce can cocktail
vegetable juice

¾ cup water

1 4-ounce can mushrooms,
undrained

½ cup ripe olives, halved

1 cup chopped celery

1 cup chopped onion

½ teaspoon salt

¼ teaspoon pepper

1 teaspoon marjoram

1 teaspoon sugar

¹⁄₁₆ teaspoon saffron

1 cup frozen peas, thawed

1 large tomato, peeled and cut
in wedges

Salt chicken. Heat ¼ cup oil in a large skillet and brown chicken slowly. While chicken browns, heat 1 tablespoon oil in a large saucepan. Add rice and garlic. Brown rice slowly, stirring occasionally. Stir in vegetable juice, water, mushrooms, ripe olives, celery, onion, salt, pepper, marjoram, sugar and saffron. Bring to a boil. Remove from heat and pour into a 9" x 13" baking pan. Place chicken pieces on top and cover lightly with aluminum foil. Dish may be made ahead to this point and refrigerated. Bake in a 350 degree oven for 1 hour, turning chicken after 30 minutes. Remove cover, sprinkle peas around chicken, top with tomato wedges, salt and pepper and bake 15 minutes longer.
6 servings.

HERBED CHICKEN WITH WINE

8-12 chicken pieces

2 teaspoons dried parsley

1 teaspoon chicken bouillon granules

½ teaspoon oregano

½ teaspoon curry powder

½ cup dry white wine

Remove skin and fat from chicken. Place in a lightly greased baking pan just large enough to hold all the pieces. Combine remaining ingredients, mix well and pour over chicken. Cover tightly and bake in a 350 degree oven for 1 hour or until chicken is done.
4-6 servings.

CHICKEN CHESTNUT

9 slices thick white bread

4 cups cooked chicken, cubed

1 8-ounce can sliced mushrooms, drained

¼ cup margarine, melted

1 8-ounce can sliced water chestnuts, drained

9 slices sharp Cheddar cheese

½ cup mayonnaise

4 eggs, well beaten

2 cups milk

1 teaspoon salt

1 can cream of mushroom soup

1 can cream of celery soup

1 2-ounce jar chopped pimento, drained

2 cups buttered coarse bread crumbs

Line a buttered 9" x 13" baking dish with bread slices. Top with chicken. Sauté mushrooms in margarine and spoon over chicken. Top with water chestnuts and cheese. Combine mayonnaise, eggs, milk and salt, beating well. Pour over cheese. Combine soups and pimento, stirring well. Spoon over casserole. Cover with foil and refrigerate 8 hours or overnight. Bake uncovered in a 350 degree oven for 30 minutes. Top with bread crumbs and return to oven for 15-20 minutes.
8-10 servings.

FESTIVE CHICKEN BUFFET

4	tablespoons butter
1	tablespoon oil
3	chicken breasts, boned, skinned and split
8	ounces fresh mushrooms, sliced
1	tablespoon flour
1	10¾ ounce can cream of chicken soup, undiluted
1	cup sherry
1	cup water
8	ounces heavy cream
Salt to taste	
½	teaspoon tarragon
¼	teaspoon pepper
2	15-ounce cans artichoke hearts, drained
8	green onions, chopped, including green part
2	tablespoons parsley, chopped
2	cups mozzarella cheese, shredded

Sauté chicken until brown on both sides in butter and oil. Remove to a 9" x 13" pan. In the same frying pan, sauté mushrooms; stir in flour. Add soup, sherry and water. Simmer until sauce thickens. Stir in cream, salt, tarragon and pepper. Mix in artichokes, onions and parsley. Mix with chicken breasts. Bake 350 degrees for 1 hour. Sprinkle with cheese and bake 5-10 minutes until cheese melts. Serve over rice. Serves 6.

CHICKEN BALTIMORE

¾	cup cooked chicken, diced
¾	cup crabmeat, chunked
1	can cream of mushroom soup
1	can cream of chicken soup
½	cup milk
1	tablespoon grated onion
½	teaspoon paprika
⅓	cup fresh mushrooms, sliced
1	tablespoon butter
½	cup buttered bread crumbs

In a saucepan mix the two soups, milk, onion and paprika and heat until just under boiling. Stir in the chicken and crabmeat. Lightly sauté the mushrooms in butter and add to the chicken mixture, blending well. Pour into a medium sized casserole, top with crumbs and bake in a 325 degree oven for 20 minutes or until brown and bubbly. Serve over rice or biscuits.
4-5 servings.

EASY CHICKEN ENCHILADAS

3-4	cups cooked chicken, cubed
1	medium onion, sliced
6	ounces Monterey Jack cheese, shredded
1	4-ounce can chopped green chilies, optional
3-4	tablespoons chicken broth
10-12	small flour tortillas
1	can cream of mushroom soup
½	cup picante sauce
2	cups Cheddar cheese, shredded

Combine chicken, onion and Monterey Jack cheese, adding chilies if desired. Stir in broth to moisten. Microwave tortillas to soften, following package directions. Put ½ cup of chicken filling on each tortilla, roll up and place seam side down in a lightly buttered 9" x 13" baking dish. Combine the mushroom soup, picante sauce and Cheddar cheese. Spread over the tortillas. Heat in a 350 degree oven until hot and bubbly or microwave until heated through.
5-6 servings.

GRILLED DUCK WITH PLUM SAUCE

Hickory chips

4-5 pound duckling

6-8 green onions with tops cut up

6   sprigs parsley

1   clove garlic, minced

½   cup soy sauce

2   tablespoons honey

2   tablespoons lemon juice

PLUM SAUCE:

1   16 ounce can purple plums

¼   teaspoon grated orange peel

3   tablespoons orange juice

2   tablespoons sugar

½   teaspoon Worcestershire sauce

¼   teaspoon ground cinnamon

Soak the hickory chips in enough water to cover, about an hour before cooking. Drain chips.

Stuff cavity of duckling with onion, parsley and garlic. Skewer neck and body cavities closed; tie legs to tail securely with cord. In saucepan, heat soy sauce, honey and lemon juice. In covered grill, arrange slow coals around edge of grill. Sprinkle coals with some of the dampened chips. Center foil pan on grill, not directly over coals. Place duck breast up in foil pan. Lower grill hood. Grill for 2¼ to 2½ hours. Sprinkle chips over coals every 30 minutes. Brush duck often with soy mixture. Remove drippings from pan as needed. Serve with plum sauce.
Serves 2-3.

Plum Sauce:
Drain the plums, reserving ¼ cup syrup. Force plums through a sieve. In a saucepan combine the sieved plums and remaining ingredients. Heat to boiling; reduce heat and simmer 10 minutes.

MEATS

PEPPER STEAK

2	pounds round steak, cut into strips 2" x ⅛"
3	tablespoons olive oil
	Garlic powder
2	green peppers, cut in strips
1	medium onion, sliced
1	1-pound can tomatoes
1	beef bouillon cube
1	tablespoon cornstarch
¼	cup water
3	tablespoons soy sauce
1	teaspoon sugar
	Salt and pepper to taste

Sprinkle garlic powder over round steak and sauté in oil until browned. Remove meat; add onion and green pepper and sauté 2 minutes. Remove peppers and onions from pan and reserve. Return meat to pan along with tomatoes and bouillon cube. Simmer, covered, 30-45 minutes until beef is tender. Blend together remaining ingredients in a cup and whip until smooth with a fork. Add sauce, green peppers and onions to meat about 5-10 minutes before serving. Stir until thickened over medium heat. Serve over rice or noodles.
Serves 6.

YANKEE POT ROAST

	5-6 pounds chuck or round roast
2	cups red wine
2	cups tomato juice
1	large onion, finely chopped
1	clove garlic, minced
½	cup dark brown sugar
2	bay leaves
	Salt and pepper to taste
¼	teaspoon nutmeg

Place the meat in a heavy roasting pan with a tight fitting lid. Mix the remaining ingredients and pour over meat. Cook in a preheated 225 degree oven for about 1 hour per pound of meat, turning meat half way through the cooking time. Remove from pan and keep warm. Thicken the pan juices for gravy. Serve surrounded by peas, carrots, potatoes or other vegetables of your choice.
8-10 servings.

SWEDISH POT ROAST

4	pounds beef (round or chuck)
1	teaspoon allspice
2	teaspoons salt
½	teaspoon pepper
3	tablespoons olive oil
¼	cup brandy
2	medium onions, sliced
⅓	cup hot bouillon
4	anchovy fillets or 1½ teaspoons anchovy paste
2	bay leaves
2	tablespoons white vinegar
2	tablespoons molasses or dark syrup
2	tablespoons heavy cream

Rub meat all over with allspice, salt and pepper. Brown meat on all sides in oil. Pour brandy over hot meat and flame. Add onions, hot bouillon, anchovies, bay leaves, vinegar and molasses and blend. Simmer tightly covered over low heat about 2 hours, or until meat is tender. Remove meat to a platter and keep warm. Make gravy by stirring cream into pan juices. Slice meat and surround on platter with browned potatoes and seasonal vegetables. Serve gravy on top of meat and/or in separate bowl. Serves 6.

POT ROAST IN BEER

3	pounds pot roast
3	tablespoons sugar
2	teaspoons salt
15	whole cloves
¼	teaspoon cayenne
Rind of 1 lemon, grated	
Rind of 1 orange, grated	
1	bottle beer
½	cup olive oil
1	large onion, chopped

In mixing bowl, combine sugar, salt, cloves, cayenne, grated lemon rind and grated orange rind. Add enough beer to make a paste. Then add olive oil and stir vigorously. Stir in remaining beer and the onion. Mix well. Place in jar and allow to stand at least 24 hours then refrigerate until ready to use.

Place roast in baking pan with tight cover. Pour 1½ cups marinade over meat. Cover and let stand 3 or 4 hours turning occasionally. Drain liquid. Sprinkle meat with ¼ teaspoon black pepper and salt to taste. Brown roast over high heat. Add the marinade liquid drained from meat; cover pot and simmer for 2½ hours or until meat is tender. Serve with a green salad, popovers, and beer.
Serves 6-8.

ISHPEMING PASTY

CRUST:

3   cups flour

¼   cup lard or shortening

1   cup suet, finely chopped

1   teaspoon salt

6-7 tablespoons cold water

FILLING:

1½ pounds lean pork, beef, or
    a combination

1   rutabaga

3   carrots

1   large onion

4   pototoes

4-5 sprigs parsley

Salt and pepper to taste

4-5 tablespoons butter or suet

To make crust, cut lard into flour and salt, using a pastry cutter. Add suet and work into the dough thoroughly. Add cold water as needed to make a soft dough. (This should be a little more moist than ordinary pastry dough.) Roll dough into 5 or 6 portions.

To fill the pasties, cut the meat and vegetables into ½" cubes. Top each piece of dough with layers of rutabaga, carrots, onion, potatoes and meat. Add some parsley, salt and pepper. Top with a pat of butter or piece of suet. Fold the dough over to make a turnover. Crimp edges and cut a slit in the top of the dough. Place pasties on a baking sheet and bake in a 400 degree oven for 45 minutes or until brown and bubbly.
Makes 5-6 servings.

The pasty is a popular treat in Michigan's Upper Peninsula. This dish originated with the miners who came from Cornwall to work in the iron ore mines.

ROLLED ROUND STEAK

2	pounds round steak, trimmed and boned
	Salt and pepper
1	pound ground beef
1	small onion, chopped
1	egg
1	tablespoon chili powder

SAUCE:

1	teaspoon Italian seasoning
3	stalks celery, chopped
1	large onion, chopped
½	pound mushrooms, sliced
1	14-ounce can stewed tomatoes
1	8-ounce can tomato purée
¾	cup red wine

Season meat with salt and pepper; tenderize with a mallet. Combine ground beef, onion, egg and chili powder. Mix well and spread on steak. Roll up and tie with heavy twine, starting at the bone end. Place steak roll in a covered baking dish.

Mix all sauce ingredients together and pour over steak. Bake 1½ hours at 350 degrees. You may add potatoes and carrots and bake an additional 30 minutes.
Serves 6.

SAUERBRATEN

5	pounds round steak, 2" thick
¾	cup vinegar
2-3	carrots, sliced
2	medium onions, chopped
1	bay leaf
5	tablespoons margarine
4	tablespoons flour
Salt and pepper to taste	
3-4 tablespoons sour cream	

Mix the vinegar, 2 cups of water, carrots, onion and bay leaf in a shallow glass baking dish. Add meat and marinate overnight, covered, in the refrigerator. When ready to cook, remove meat from marinade and set marinade aside. In a large heavy skillet or Dutch oven, brown the meat in the margarine. Remove meat from pan and stir in flour. Cook until flour browns; do not burn. Add 2 cups of water and two cups of the marinade. Season with salt and pepper, bring to a boil and cook, stirring, until thickened. Reduce heat to a simmer. Remove the onions, carrots and bay leaf from marinade and add to the pan, along with the meat. Add more water if gravy is too thick or does not cover the meat. Simmer, covered, for 4 hours. Remove meat from gravy, cool and slice. Remove bay leaf and thicken gravy if needed. Adjust seasonings. Stir in sour cream. Return meat to pan and warm; do not boil. Serve with KIM'S RED CABBAGE.
6 servings.

BEEF TIPS ITALIAN

3	pounds lean stew meat
Salt and pepper to taste	
2	tablespoons olive oil
1½	cups water
1	12-ounce can tomatoes
½	teaspoon sugar
1	teaspoon oregano
2	carrots, thinly sliced
2	cloves garlic, minced
1	tablespoon lemon juice

Sprinkle meat with salt and pepper and brown in oil. Combine remaining ingredients and pour over meat. Cover and simmer 1½-2 hours until meat is tender. Serve over rice, sprinkled with Parmesan cheese. Serves 6-8.

GOURMET BEEF BRISKET

4-5 pound beef brisket, trimmed	
Salt and pepper to taste	
1	package oxtail soup mix
½	jar red currant jelly
¾	cup red wine

Lay the brisket on a double layer of foil. Season with salt and pepper to taste. Bring up the sides of the foil, add ½ cup water and seal foil. Place in a covered roasting pan and cook in a 250 degree oven for 4-5 hours, or until fork tender. Pour juices off into a bowl, adding water to make 2½ cups of liquid. Cover and refrigerate both the juices and the meat for 24 hours. Before servings, slice the chilled brisket ⅛" - ¼" thick. Layer the slices in a shallow baking dish. Put the juices, the oxtail soup mix, the jelly and the wine in a saucepan, bring to a boil and pour over the meat. Cover and bake in a 350 degree for ½ hour, or until heated through.
8 servings.

TOURNEDOS BORDELAISE

4	tournedos (beef tenderloin cut 1-1½" thick)
Salt	
1	tablespoon butter
1	tablespoon shallots, finely minced
½	cup dry red wine
¾	cup homemade gravy
1	tablespoon fresh lemon juice
2	tablespoons parsley, minced
½	cup fresh mushrooms, sliced
2	teaspoons butter
Salt and cayenne pepper	

Broil or grill meat 4-5 minutes; 9 minutes for medium. Season with salt if desired. Turn and broil an additional 4-5 minutes for rare; 7-8 for medium. Season second side with salt if desired.

To make sauce, melt 1 tablespoon butter, add shallots and sauté until soft. Add wine and simmer until reduced to half its volume. Stir in gravy, lemon juice, parsley and mushrooms which have been sautéed in 2 teaspoons butter. Season with salt and cayenne to taste. Heat through before serving. Serves 4.

MEATLOAF WELLINGTON

1½	pounds lean ground round
1	egg
2	tablespoons dried onion
½	cup mushroom gravy, canned or homemade
½	cup red wine
1	tablespoon parsley, chopped
⅔	cup soft bread crumbs
Salt and pepper to taste	
1	package refrigerated crescent shaped rolls

Mix ground meat, egg, onion, gravy, wine, parsley, bread crumbs, salt and pepper. Add more wine or crumbs, if necessary, to achieve desired consistency. Pat mixture into a firm rectangle in a 9" x 13" pan, leaving space on all sides. Bake in a 350 degree oven for 45 minutes. Pour off any accumulated fat. Separate rolls and overlap over the top of the meatloaf. Return to the oven and continue to cook for 15 minutes or until golden brown. Using two spatulas, remove meatloaf to a platter. Slice and serve with additional mushroom gravy or ONION SAUCE.

STUFFED PIZZA

2	16-ounce loaves frozen bread dough, thawed
1½	pounds ground beef, pork or Italian sausage
1	medium onion, thinly sliced
½	pound fresh mushrooms, sliced
1	cup grated Parmesan cheese
10	ounces mozzarella cheese, sliced
1	green pepper, sliced into rings
1	15½ ounce jar extra thick spaghetti sauce
2	teaspoons dried thyme
2	teaspoons dried fennel seed, crushed
Milk	
2	tablespoons cornmeal

Shape dough into 2 balls, cover and let rise until nearly doubled. Punch down, cover and let rest 10 minutes.

In a large skillet, cook ground meat and onion until brown. Remove meat with a slotted spoon and pour off fat. Sauté mushrooms; set aside.

On floured surface, roll half of dough to a 14" circle. Grease a 12" pizza pan and sprinkle it with cornmeal. Fit dough into pan and sprinkle with ½ cup Parmesan. Top with meat-onion mixture, mushrooms, mozzarella cheese slices and green pepper. Spoon spaghetti sauce over and sprinkle with thyme, fennel and remaining Parmesan cheese. Roll remaining dough to 13" circle and place on top of filling. Fold extra bottom crust down and pinch to top crust to seal. Cut small slits in top of crust. Bake at 400 degrees for 15 minutes. Brush with milk, sprinkle with cornmeal. Bake 15 minutes more or until the top is well browned. Let stand 15 minutes before serving.
Serves 10.

PIZZA BURGERS

1½ pounds ground beef

½   cup green pepper, diced

½   cup onion, diced

½   cup stuffed olives, diced

¾   pound sharp Cheddar cheese, diced

1   can tomato soup

Hamburger buns

Brown and drain ground beef; set aside to cool. Dice vegetables and cheese; mix with ground beef; stir in soup. Spread on halves of hamburger buns. Bake open faced on a cookie sheet in a 375 degree oven for 15 minutes. May be put on small party rolls and used as an appetizer.
Serves 6-8.

JUDY'S JOES

3   pounds beef stew meat

32 ounces ketchup

1   tablespoon vinegar

1   teaspoon ground cloves

1   teaspoon ginger

1   teaspoon allspice

3   tablespoons dried onion

Put meat in roasting pan; add 1 cup of water and remaining ingredients. Mix well. Cover and cook 3 hours in a 300 degree oven. Shred meat with two forks. Serve on buns.

MEATS

BETTER BURGERS

1	egg
2	tablespoons Italian seasoning
½	cup chopped onion
¼	cup chopped olives
Garlic, salt, pepper to taste	
2	pounds ground beef
½	cup oil based Italian dressing

Put egg in mixing bowl and beat; add the seasonings, onions, olives and beef. Mix well and shape into 6 to 8 patties. These are best if refrigerated several hours before grilling. Cook on hot grill, basting with dressing. Serve on a bun.

You can add other spices to your heart's content!

HAM BARBEQUE

½	cup onion, chopped
¾	cup water
2	tablespoons Worcestershire sauce
1	teaspoon paprika
¾	cup ketchup
2	tablespoons vinegar
2	tablespoons brown sugar
1	teaspoon chili powder
2	pounds shaved ham

Place ham in a small covered roasting pan. Combine all other ingredients to make sauce. Pour barbecue over ham and bake for 1 to 1½ hours in a 300 degree oven. Stir occasionally. Serve on hamburger buns.
Makes 8-10.

MEDITERRANEAN STEW

3	medium potatoes, peeled and cubed
4	medium carrots, peeled and sliced
2	medium onions, cut in chunks
1	pound beef stew meat
1	8-ounce can tomato sauce
1	cup dry red wine
1	tablespoon brown sugar
¼	teaspoon salt
2	tablespoons wine vinegar
¼	teaspoon cumin
⅛	teaspoon garlic powder
⅛	teaspoon pepper
¼	cup raisins
1	1" piece of stick cinnamon, sliced
½	teaspoon whole cloves
1	bay leaf

In a 3½ quart slow cooker, place the potatoes, carrots, onions, and stew meat. In bowl combine the tomato sauce, wine, brown sugar, salt, vinegar, cumin, garlic powder and pepper. Stir in the raisins, stick cinnamon, cloves and bay leaf. Pour the mixture over meat in cooker. Cover and cook on high heat for 5-6 or on low heat 10-12 hours, or until tender. Remove cinnamon, cloves and bay leaf before serving. Serves 3-4.

MULLIGAN STEW

1½	pounds ground chuck
1	medium onion, chopped
1	eggplant, peeled and chopped
1	clove garlic, minced
½	cup carrots, sliced
½	cup celery, sliced
1	teaspoon salt
1	teaspoon sugar
2	tablespoons oil
1	12-ounce can tomatoes with liquid
2	14-ounce cans beef broth
½	teaspoon pepper
½	teaspoon nutmeg
½	cup elbow macaroni

Sauté the first 8 ingredients together in the oil. Then add the tomatoes, beef broth, pepper and nutmeg. Cover, bring to a boil and simmer 2 hours. During the last hour add the macaroni.
Serves 4.

MILLION DOLLAR MEATBALLS

2   eggs, beaten

1¼ cups soft bread crumbs

1   cup Parmesan cheese, grated

½   10-ounce package frozen
    chopped spinach, thawed and
    squeezed dry

1½-2 pounds ground beef

3   tablespoons vegetable oil

1   tablespoon lemon juice

2   envelopes brown gravy mix

2¼ cups water

Combine eggs, bread crumbs, and
cheese in a bowl. Add spinach and
beef and mix well. Shape into
meatballs and brown in oil. Remove
meatballs from pan, set aside and
keep warm. Drain excess oil from
pan and stir in 2¼ cups water,
lemon juice and gravy mix. Cook
2-3 minutes, or until thickened.
Return meatballs to pan and cook
15-20 minutes, or until cooked
through.
4-6 servings.

SHERRIED PORK TENDERLOIN

1½ pounds pork tenderloin,
    fat trimmed

¼   cup flour

Seasoned salt and pepper to taste

2   tablespoons butter

1   medium onion, sliced

8   ounces mushrooms, sliced

½   cup dry sherry

½   teaspoon dried rosemary,
    crushed

½   cup sliced green pimento-
    stuffed olives

Slice pork into 1" slices; dredge in
flour seasoned with salt and
pepper. Melt butter in a large skillet
and sauté pork and onion until
pork is browned. Stir in
mushrooms, sherry and rosemary.
Cover and simmer over low heat
until pork is thoroughly cooked
and tender, 30-40 minutes.
Stir in olives.
4 servings.

MEATS

CROWN ROAST OF PORK

5-7 pound crown roast of pork (12-14 ribs)
½ teaspoon salt
¼ teaspoon black pepper
1 jar red currant jelly
½ cup apple brandy
3 cups chicken broth
8 tablespoons butter
1½ cups uncooked brown rice
2 cups chopped red apples
¾ cup golden raisins
¾ cup celery, chopped
½ cup pecans, chopped
1½ tablespoons parsley, chopped
1 teaspoon thyme
1 small onion, chopped
Apple slices as garnish

Preheat oven to 325 degrees. Salt and pepper inside of roast; place roast in a shallow roaster, bone side up, cover rib tips with aluminum foil. Heat jelly and ¼ cup apple brandy. Brush over roast and reserve remainder of mixture for sauce. Bake 30-35 minutes per pound or until a meat thermometer reads 170 degrees. Baste every 15 minutes.

After 30 minutes of roasting, bring broth and 6 tablespoons butter to boil in saucepan; stir in rice, apples, raisins, celery, pecans, parsley and thyme. Reduce heat to low and simmer covered 1-1½ hours until rice is tender. Remove from heat and stir in remaining brandy. About 30 minutes before roast is done fill center of roast with a portion of rice mixture. Place remaining rice in covered baking dish in oven.

To make red currant sauce, combine remaining 2 tablespoons butter and onion in a small skillet and sauté until soft; strain to remove onion if desired. Add remaining basting mixture to butter and heat until bubbly.

To serve, remove foil from tips and place roast on serving platter with rice. Garnish with apple slices and serve with red currant sauce on the side.
Serves 8-10.

See photo illustration.

TIPSY PORK CHOPS

6-8 pork chops

½ **cup bourbon**

½ **cup soy sauce**

½ **cup molasses**

¼ **cup Dijon mustard**

½ **cup boiling water**

3 **cloves garlic, crushed**

½ **teaspoon cayenne**

¼ **teaspoon black pepper**

Combine all ingredients, except pork chops, and stir well to make marinade. Pour the marinade over pork chops and marinate for 24 hours. Drain marinade and save. Brown pork chops in a skillet. Place chops in baking dish; pour reserved marinade over chops and bake covered at 350 degrees for 45 minutes. May need to add water if too dry.
Serves 6.

BLACK FOREST PORK CHOPS

4 **pork loin chops, 1½" thick**

Salt and pepper

2 **tablespoons oil**

1 **ounce Kirsch, heated**

¼ **cup beef stock**

1 **16-ounce can pitted dark cherries**

½ **teaspoon each nutmeg, cloves, marjoram**

½ **teaspoon grated lemon rind**

2 **tablespoons lemon juice**

2 **teaspoons cornstarch**

1 **teaspoon beef bouillon granules**

½ **cup chopped toasted walnuts**

Trim fat from chops and season with salt and pepper. Heat oil in skillet over medium heat; add chops and cook until brown on both sides. Drain fat from pan and flambé chops with heated Kirsch. Pour in stock, cover and simmer over low heat for 1 hour.

Drain syrup from cherries; reserve both. Add seasonings and lemon rind to syrup; stir lemon juice and cornstarch together and slowly add to syrup mixture. Cook over low heat until sauce is thick and glossy. Stir in bouillon. After chops have cooked 45 minutes, pour syrup mixture into pan with chops.

Just before serving, add reserved cherries and walnuts and cook over low heat until warmed through.
Serves 4.

RIBS MAUI

2	pounds baby back ribs
Salt and pepper	
1	8-ounce can tomato sauce
½	cup brown sugar
½	cup sherry
½	cup honey
2	tablespoons wine vinegar
2	tablespoons onion, minced
¼	teaspoon Worcestershire sauce
1½	tablespoons cornstarch
½	cup water

Salt and pepper spareribs. Place in shallow baking pan and bake at 400 degrees for 40 minutes. In saucepan combine other ingredients except cornstarch and water. Bring to a boil. Mix cornstarch and water together and add to hot mixture. Stir until thickened and translucent. Brush sauce over ribs and continue baking ribs at 350 degrees for an additional hour or until tender, basting with sauce frequently.

MARINATED BUTTERFLIED LEG OF LAMB

1	5-6 pound leg of lamb, boned, trimmed and butterflied
1	cup olive oil
1	medium onion, sliced
½	cup dry white wine
⅓	cup fresh lemon juice
⅓	cup chopped fresh parsley
3	garlic cloves, minced
1½	tablespoons dried rosemary, crumbled
3	teaspoons Dijon mustard
½	teaspoon salt and pepper

Combine all ingredients, except lamb, in a bowl and mix well. Place the lamb in a large flat non-aluminum pan or salad bowl. Pour marinade over the lamb, cover and refrigerate overnight, turning several times.

Prepare grill. Place lamb on grill, cook 15 minutes per side for rare meat or until desired doneness is reached. Baste with marinade. May serve with GARLIC GRILLED VEGETABLE POCKETS.
Serves 8.

MEATS

LAMB SHANKS à la ROSE MARIE

8	lamb shanks
2	garlic cloves, peeled
⅛	teaspoon thyme
⅛	teaspoon rosemary
2	cups white wine
2	tablespoons cornstarch
Chopped chives	
Black pepper to taste	
Lemon slices for garnish	

Have the lamb shanks at room temperature. Rub each shank with raw garlic on both sides; sprinkle shanks with thyme and rosemary. Place meat on a rack in a covered roasting pan. Bake in preheated 250 degree oven for 1½-2 hours. When cooked, wrap shanks in foil and refrigerate until the next day. Pour pan juices in a container and refrigerate. Before using juices discard solidified fat.

Next day, pour pan juices in a large skillet; add shanks and 2 cups wine. Heat for 30 minutes or until hot. Thicken juices with cornstarch, sprinkle with chives and pepper and top with lemon slices.
Makes 4 servings.

SPOON LAMB

2-3 tablespoons olive oil

2   carrots, sliced

1   onion, sliced

5-7 pound leg of lamb, skin, fat and bone removed

1   bay leaf

1-2 sprigs parsley

1   cup beef stock

Juice of 2 limes

½   cup soy sauce

1   cup sherry, or red wine

¼   cup Worcestershire sauce

2   tablespoons cornstarch

Preheat oven to 375 degrees. Rub the lamb with a small amount of olive oil. Heat remaining oil in a covered roasting pan. Add carrots and onion, stirring to coat with oil. Put lamb, bay leaf, parsley and beef stock in pan and brown in the oven for 20-30 minutes. Reduce heat to 325 degrees. Mix together the lime juice, soy sauce, sherry and Worcestershire sauce; pour over the lamb. Bake covered 4-6 hours, or until the meat falls apart. Baste with pan juices at least every 30 minutes throughout cooking time. When lamb is done, remove it to a serving platter. Press the cooking juices and vegetables through a sieve into a saucepan. Mix cornstarch with 3-4 tablespoons water or sherry and add to the juice. Cook, stirring, over medium heat until thickened. Pour sauce over meat and serve with a spoon. 6 servings.

VEAL PATTIES

1   pound ground veal

3   slices bacon, cut fine

1   cup stuffing mix

1   egg, well beaten

½   medium onion, chopped

Salt, pepper and garlic powder to taste

1   can cream of mushroom soup

Combine first 6 ingredients for patties and mix well; sauté in vegetable oil. Mix together soup and drippings; pour over patties in a baking dish and bake 1 hour at 350 degrees.
Serves 2-3.

VEAL DELIGHT

1½	pounds veal cut into 1" cubes
4	tablespoons flour
1	teaspoon salt
⅛	teaspoon black pepper
4	tablespoons olive oil
1½	cup onions, sliced thin
8-10	ounces fresh mushrooms, sliced
¾	cup sour cream

Dredge meat in flour, salt and pepper. Sauté onions and mushrooms in oil and cook until tender. Remove onions and mushrooms from skillet; add meat and brown. Place meat in a 2-quart casserole, cover with onions and mushrooms. Add sour cream and bake in a 325 degrees oven until meat is just tender, 35-40 minutes. May be made in morning and heated just before serving. Do not overcook or sour cream will curdle. Serve with rice or noodles. Serves 4-6.

CURRIED VEAL

3-4	tablespoons margarine
3	pounds veal for stew
1	cup onion, sliced
1	cup celery, diced
3	large apples, peeled and cut into ½" wedges
2	teaspoons curry powder
1½	teaspoons salt
3	tablespoons flour
2	cups water

Melt margarine in frying pan. Sauté veal until browned; transfer to a large baking dish. In the same skillet, sauté apples until softened. Spoon apples over veal. Sauté onion and celery until soft and spread over apples. Add 1 tablespoon margarine to the frying pan. When it is melted, stir in salt, curry powder and flour. Slowly add 2 cups of water, stirring constantly. Cook, stirring until thickened. Pour over veal, cover tightly and bake in a 350 degree oven for 45 minutes to 1 hour. Serve with rice or noodles. 8 servings.

VEAL EN CROÛTE

8	veal medallions, about 6 ounces each
8	tablespoons unsalted butter
8	tablespoons shallots, chopped
48	large spinach leaves, stems removed and blanched
8	pieces puff pastry
1	egg, beaten
16	shrimps, cooked and deveined
8	mushroom caps, sautéed

SAUCE:

1½	cups chicken or veal stock
1	cup dry white wine
Juice of 1 lemon	
1	teaspoon thyme
1	teaspoon tarragon
Salt and pepper	
1	cup heavy cream

Sauté veal in butter, browning on both sides; reserve. In same pan, sauté shallots and divide atop veal medallions. Top each with leaves of spinach. Wrap each in puff pastry; seal bottom. Wash with egg. If you cool meat first, it may be prepared to this point and refrigerated until ready to bake.

When ready to bake, place in preheated 425 degree oven for 15 minutes or until pastry is brown. Meanwhile make sauce by deglazing frying pan with stock. Add wine, lemon juice and seasonings.

Reduce sauce. Add cream and pass through a sieve.

To serve, top each piece with 2 shrimp and 1 mushroom cap. Spoon sauce over top.

Chicken breasts may be used in place of veal.
Serves 8.

MEATS

MARINADE FOR FLANK STEAK I

1   cup vegetable oil

½   cup soy sauce

¼   cup green onions, minced

1   clove garlic, pressed

½-⅔ cup gin

Dash of grated fresh ginger or
    powdered ginger

Mix all ingredients and pour over
flank steak. Marinate 6 hours or
overnight. Broil or grill meat,
basting with marinade.

MARINADE FOR FLANK STEAK II

½   cup soy sauce

¾-1 cup vegetable oil

3   teaspoons honey

2   teaspoons vinegar

1   clove garlic, minced

Freshly ground pepper

Mix ingredients and marinate flank
steak for at least 4 hours, turning
several times. Broil 4-5 minutes per
side for medium rare.

FRANKLY GREAT SAUCE

1   cup sour cream

1   tablespoon prepared mustard

1   tablespoon chopped onion

Chopped chives or green onion
    tops to taste

Mix all of the ingredients together.
Blend thoroughly. Super on
frankfurters.

ONION SAUCE

2	tablespoons butter
1 - 1½	tablespoons sugar
1	tablespoon flour
6	small onions, sliced thin
1	10½ ounce can consommé
1	tablespoon vinegar
Salt	

Stir sugar into melted butter until carmelized. Add flour, stir until smooth, then add sliced onions, consommé, vinegar and salt to taste. When mixture begins to bubble, turn temperature to low and continue to cook for 20 minutes, stirring frequently. Great with meatloaf.

ANCHOVY BUTTER

½	cup (1 stick) unsalted butter, room temperature
4	anchovy fillets, rinsed, drained and chopped
1	teaspoon fresh lemon juice
Dash of hot pepper sauce	

Combine all ingredients in small bowl. Mix well. Dollop on cooked steaks or pass separately. Makes about ½ cup.

SHALLOT - TARRAGON BUTTER

½	cup (1 stick) unsalted butter, room temperature
3	shallots, minced
1 - 2 teaspoons dried, finely crumbled tarragon	
Salt and freshly ground pepper	

Combine all ingredients in small bowl. Mix well. Dollop on cooked steaks or pass separately. Makes about ½ cup.

VEGETABLES

VEGETABLES

ASPARAGUS MARY ELIZABETH

1	pound fresh asparagus
1	tablespoon sugar
1	tablespoon butter, softened

Cut the asparagus diagonally into 1" pieces. Heap along the edges of a large heavy skillet, leaving the center clear. Add sugar to the center of the skillet, increase heat and cook until sugar melts and turns brown at the edges. Put the butter in the middle of the sugar. Quickly cover the skillet and shake vigorously to coat the asparagus with the butter and sugar mixture. Cook, covered, on high heat for 1 minute. Remove from heat and let rest for 2-3 minutes. Serve hot. 4 servings.

ASPARAGUS WITH ORANGE HOLLANDAISE

2	egg yolks
2	tablespoons orange juice, preferably fresh
1½	teaspoons grated orange peel
Salt and pepper to taste	
5	tablespoons butter
¼	cup sour cream
2	pounds fresh asparagus, cooked crisp-tender

Combine egg yolks, orange juice, orange peel, salt and pepper in a heavy saucepan. Place pan over low heat and whisk in butter, 1 tablespoon at a time until butter is melted and sauce thickens. Remove from heat and stir in sour cream. Pour sauce over hot, cooked asparagus and garnish with additional orange peel. 6-8 servings.

MARINATED ASPARAGUS

1	cup wine vinegar
½	cup water
½	cup salad oil
1½	tablespoons oregano
1	tablespoon salt
2	cloves garlic, minced
1	tablespoon Accent
1	pound asparagus, cooked

Mix first 7 ingredients together and pour over asparagus. Marinate for 6 hours or overnight. Serve chilled.

CITRUS BEETS

2	pounds of fresh beets
	Juice and grated peel of 1 lemon
1	tablespoon grated orange peel
2½	tablespoons sugar
½	teaspoon salt
½	teaspoon ground cloves
2	tablespoons frozen orange juice concentrate
1½	tablespoons cornstarch
1	tablespoon butter or margarine

Simmer beets in water until tender; reserve cooking liquid. Peel and slice beets; set aside. Pour 1½ cups of the cooking liquid into a saucepan. Add the lemon juice, lemon peel, orange peel, sugar, salt, cloves and orange juice concentrate, stirring to combine. Dissolve the cornstarch in 2-3 tablespoons water and add to the saucepan. Cook, stirring until sauce is thickened and clear. Add the sliced beets and the butter. Heat through and serve.
4 servings.

BROCCOLI CUSTARD

3	bunches broccoli, cooked crisp-tender and drained
2	tablespoons flour
2	tablespoons butter
1	cup milk
1	cup mayonnaise
1	tablespoon lemon juice
½	pound Cheddar cheese, shredded

Chop broccoli and measure 6-8 cups; set aside. Melt butter in a medium saucepan; whisk in the flour. Remove from heat and slowly add the milk, stirring. Heat gently, stirring constantly until smooth and thickened. Remove from heat and blend in the mayonnaise and lemon juice. Stir in the broccoli and turn into a buttered 2 quart casserole. Top with Cheddar cheese. Place casserole in a larger shallow pan and pour in hot water half way up the sides of the casserole. Bake in a 325 degree oven for 45 minutes or until set. 8 servings.

DEVILED BRUSSELS SPROUTS

2	10-ounce packages frozen Brussels sprouts, thawed
3	tablespoons vegetable oil
2	tablespoons Dijon mustard
¼	teaspoon salt
¼	cup water

Cut each sprout in half lengthwise. In a Dutch oven over high heat cook the sprouts in oil for 5 minutes. Add the mustard, salt and water. Reduce heat to medium, cover and cook 5 minutes more, stirring occasionally. 6 servings.

KIM'S RED CABBAGE

2	medium heads red cabbage, cut into thin strips
8-10 strips of bacon	
1	tart apple, chopped
¼	cup vinegar
2	tablespoons sugar
Salt and pepper to taste	
3	tablespoons cornstarch

In a heavy skillet cook bacon until crisp; reserve bacon for another use. Add the cabbage to the drippings, along with the apple. Pour in ½ cup water, vinegar, sugar, salt and pepper. Cook, covered, over very low heat, stirring occasionally, for 2 hours. Before serving, blend cornstarch with 3-4 tablespoons of water and stir into the cabbage. Cook until thickened. 6-8 servings.

MARY MURPHY'S COLCANNON

3	pounds Idaho potatoes, peeled and quartered
4	cups kale, or cabbage, chopped
1	bunch scallions, finely chopped
8	tablespoons butter, divided
1	cup milk
Salt and pepper to taste	
Additional melted butter, as desired	

Boil the potatoes until tender. While the potatoes cook, cook the kale in 1" of water until tender, 5-10 minutes. Drain thoroughly. Melt 2 tablespoons butter in a medium skillet. Add the scallions and cook until transparent. Add the kale and cook, stirring constantly for 1-2 minutes. Cover skillet and set aside. Drain potatoes, return to pan and dry over low heat. Beat in the remaining 6 tablespoons of butter and as much milk as needed to make a thick purée. Stir in kale, scallions, salt and pepper to taste. Serve with melted butter. 6-8 servings.

COPPER COINS

2	pounds carrots, sliced and cooked tender
1	cup sugar
1	cup vegetable oil
¾	cup white vinegar
1	can condensed tomato soup
1	small onion, chopped

Combine the sugar, oil, vinegar, soup and onion in a saucepan. Simmer 5-7 minutes. Pour over carrots and marinate several hours or overnight. Serve at room temperature.

CARROTS WITH HORSERADISH SAUCE

1	pound fresh or frozen baby carrots
2	cups water
2	tablespoons prepared horseradish
2	tablespoons grated onion
1	cup mayonnaise
½	teaspoon salt
¼	teaspoon pepper
¼	cup saltine cracker crumbs
2	tablespoons butter
Paprika	

Cook the carrots in water until tender. Drain, reserving 1/4 cup of the cooking liquid. Combine the reserved liquid with the horseradish, onion, mayonnaise, salt and pepper. Place the carrots in a buttered 8" baking dish. Pour sauce over the top. Sprinkle with cracker crumbs and dot with butter. Dust with paprika. Bake in a 375 degree oven for 20 minutes. 6 servings.

CORN PIE

1	4 ounce can chopped chili peppers
1	15 ounce can creamed style corn
1	cup buttermilk baking mix
1	egg
¼	cup milk
½	cup Monterey Jack cheese, shredded

Mix first five ingredients and pour into an 8" square casserole. Sprinkle cheese on top and bake at 350 degrees, 30-40 minutes. This casserole will rise and fall. Serve in squares.

CURRIED CAULIFLOWER CASSEROLE

1	large head cauliflower, broken into flowerets, cooked and drained
1	can cream of mushroom soup
⅓	cup mayonnaise
1	teaspoon curry powder
¼	cup dried bread crumbs
2	tablespoons butter, melted

Place cauliflower in a shallow 2 quart casserole. In a small bowl stir together the soup, mayonnaise and curry powder, blending well. Pour sauce over the cauliflower. Toss bread crumbs and melted butter together and sprinkle over casserole. Bake, uncovered, in a 350 degree oven for 30 minutes, or until hot and bubbly.
6-8 servings.

VEGETABLES

CELERY WITH STILTON

10-12 stalks celery
4 tablespoons butter, divided
¼ cup flour
1½ cups milk
2 tablespoons olive oil
1 cup fresh bread crumbs
4 ounces Stilton, or other blue cheese

Slice celery diagonally and simmer in water gently until just tender. Melt 3 tablespoons butter in a small saucepan. Whisk in flour 1 tablespoon at a time. Cook, stirring 1-2 minutes. Slowly whisk in the milk and cook, stirring, until sauce is thickened; keep warm. In a small skillet melt the remaining 1 tablespoon of butter. Add the olive oil and stir in the bread crumbs; cook 2-3 minutes. Place celery in a shallow baking dish. Crumble the Stilton into the sauce, stirring until smooth. Pour sauce over the celery and sprinkle with the crumbs. Place under a broiler for 3-4 minutes, or until crumbs are browned. Dish may be prepared ahead and refrigerated. Bake in a 375 degree oven for 30 minutes, or until heated through. 6 servings.

CRISPY EGGPLANT

½ cup mayonnaise
1 tablespoon minced dried onion
¼ teaspoon salt
⅓ cup Italian flavored bread crumbs
⅓ cup Parmesan cheese, grated
1 eggplant, unpeeled or peeled, cut into ½″ slices

Mix together the mayonnaise, onion and salt. Combine bread crumbs and cheese in a shallow plate. Brush both sides of the eggplant slices with the mayonnaise mixture and coat with crumbs. Place slices on a baking sheet and cook in a 425 degree oven for 15-17 minutes, turning carefully after 8 minutes. 4-6 servings.

CREAMY EGGPLANT

1	large eggplant, peeled and cubed
1	teaspoon salt
1	can cream of mushroom soup
½	cup milk
2	eggs, beaten
1	medium onion, chopped
16	saltine crackers, crushed
Dash of pepper	
5-6 slices bacon, uncooked	

Place the eggplant in a heavy saucepan and cover with water. Add salt and simmer for 5 minutes. Drain well. Combine the soup, milk, eggs, onion, cracker crumbs and pepper in a bowl. Stir in the drained eggplant and blend well. Pour into a buttered 2 quart casserole. Cut the bacon into 2" pieces and sprinkle over casserole. Bake in a 350 degree oven for 1 hour, or until bacon is crisp. 6 servings.

DELUXE GREEN BEANS

2	cups French style green beans, cooked
⅓	cup minced onion
2	tablespoons butter
2	tablespoons flour
1	teaspoon salt
¼	teaspoon pepper
1	cup sour cream
½	cup Cheddar cheese, shredded

Simmer onion in butter. Add flour, salt and pepper. Add sour cream. Blend. Add cooked beans. Fill a buttered 1 quart shallow dish. Top with shredded cheese. Bake 350 degrees for 15 minutes.

DIJON MUSHROOMS

¼	cup butter
½	small onion, chopped
1	pound fresh mushrooms, sliced
⅓	cup dry vermouth
1	tablespoon Dijon mustard
	Salt and freshly ground black pepper to taste

Melt butter in a heavy skillet over medium heat. Add the onion and sauté until transparent. Add the mushrooms and sauté until tender, increasing heat as needed. Add vermouth and cook, stirring, until liquid is reduced by ½. Stir in the mustard. Season to taste with salt and pepper.
2-3 servings.

ONIONS EUGENE

4	medium white onions
2	tablespoons margarine
½	teaspoon nutmeg
	Salt to taste
3	tablespoons sherry
3	ounces Swiss cheese, shredded, optional
	Whole wheat or rye bread, toasted, optional

In a covered skillet over medium heat, sauté onions in butter until transparent and light golden brown. Season with nutmeg and salt while cooking. Reduce heat, add the sherry and cook until the liquid is reduced and the onions are moist. Serve hot as a side dish or heap on toast, top with Swiss cheese and broil until cheese has melted.
4 servings.

APPLE ONION BAKE

4	medium onions, sliced
2	medium tart apples, cored, peeled and sliced
2	tablespoons all purpose flour
2	tablespoons brown sugar
1	teaspoon salt
Dash pepper	
2	tablespoons butter

Combine flour, sugar, salt and pepper. Toss apple slices with flour mixture. Arrange apples and onions in alternate layers in a 2 quart casserole. Dot the top with butter. Cover and bake in a 350 degree oven for 1 hour.
6 servings.

PEAS WILLIS

¾	pound fresh mushrooms, sliced
2	tablespoons margarine
1	20 ounce bag frozen peas
1	bunch green onions, sliced
1½	cups shredded lettuce
1	tablespoon sugar
3	tablespoons heavy cream
2	teaspoons fresh parsley, chopped
Salt and pepper to taste	

Sauté mushrooms in margarine. Cook peas; drain well. Add peas plus all ingredients except lettuce, to mushrooms. When mixture is hot, add lettuce and serve when lettuce is warm.

VEGETABLES

GREEN AND RED SAUTÉ

1	pound sugar snap peas, strings removed
2	small red peppers, julienned
2	tablespoons unsalted butter
¼	teaspoon salt
Pinch of pepper	

Blanch snap peas and pepper strips in boiling water for 1 minute. Immerse in cold water to stop cooking; drain well. Melt butter in medium skillet. Add vegetables and sauté until heated through. Season with salt and pepper.
4 servings.

ROASTED RED PEPPERS

5-6 large, firm red bell peppers	
4	cloves garlic, minced
1	can flat anchovies, undrained
2	teaspoons capers
4	tablespoons fresh parsley, chopped
¼	cup olive oil
1	tablespoon wine vinegar

To roast peppers, place on a broiler pan and broil 4" - 5" from the heat, turning every 3-5 minutes. Peppers should be charred and bubbled on all sides. Remove from oven and place in a brown bag. Close bag tightly and allow peppers to steam for 10 minutes. Remove peppers from bag and peel off skins. Seed and slice into julienne strips. Place peppers and remaining ingredients in a skillet and simmer, uncovered, for 10 minutes. Cool and refrigerate. Peppers will keep for 1 week. Return to room temperature before serving.

RED ROSEMARY POTATOES

8	medium red potatoes, about 2 pounds
1	large clove garlic, minced
3	tablespoons olive oil
1¼	teaspoon dried oregano
1¼	teaspoon dried rosemary
¼	teaspoon salt
¼	teaspoon crushed red pepper flakes

Scrub and quarter potatoes; do not peel. Place potatoes in a large bowl. Add the remaining ingredients and toss to coat. Arrange the potatoes in a single layer in a jelly roll pan. Bake in a 425 degree oven for 30 minutes. Turn over and continue cooking for 15-20 minutes, or until well browned.
6 servings.

HEAVENLY HASH BROWNS

1	32-ounce package frozen hash brown potatoes
2	cans potato soup
1	pint sour cream
1	pound Cheddar cheese, shredded
	Parmesan cheese

Mix hash browns, soup, sour cream and Cheddar cheese together and turn into a buttered 9" x 13" baking dish. Sprinkle with grated Parmesan. Bake in a 350 degree oven for 1 hour, or until browned.
8 servings.

VEGETABLES

GOLDEN PARMESAN POTATOES

6	large potatoes, peeled and quartered
¼	cup sifted flour
¼	cup Parmesan cheese, grated
¾	teaspoon salt
⅛	teaspoon pepper
⅓	cup butter, melted
Chopped parsley	

Combine the flour, cheese, salt and pepper in a plastic bag. Moisten potatoes with water. Drop a few pieces at a time into the bag and shake to coat. Spread the melted butter evenly in a 9" x 13" baking pan. Arrange the coated potatoes in a single layer in the pan. Bake in a 375 degree oven for 1 hour, turning once during baking. Before serving, sprinkle with parsley.
6-8 servings.

GARLIC GRILLED VEGETABLE POCKETS

4-5	medium red potatoes, unpeeled, sliced
2	medium onions, sliced
1	red or green bell pepper, cut into strips
4	cloves garlic, chopped
3	tablespoons olive oil
2	teaspoons fresh sage, minced
Salt and pepper to taste	

Prepare grill. Toss all ingredients together in a bowl. Divide between 2 greased rectangles of heavy duty foil. Seal pockets securely. Place on edge of grill and cook until potatoes are tender, 35-40 minutes.
3-4 servings.

HUBBARD SQUASH PUDDING

4	cups Hubbard or other winter squash, peeled, seeded and coarsely shredded
½	cup water
2	tablespoons butter
1	teaspoon salt, divided
3	eggs
¼	cup brown sugar, firmly packed
½	teaspoon cinnamon, nutmeg or ginger
¼	teaspoon pepper

In a heavy saucepan, bring the water to a boil; add the butter and ½ teaspoon salt. Stir in the squash and simmer, covered, for 5 minutes, or until the squash is tender and the water is absorbed. Mash the squash. Measure 2 cups and set aside. In a medium bowl whisk together the eggs, sugar, cinnamon, pepper and remaining ½ teaspoon salt. Stir in the 2 cups of mashed squash and blend well. Pour into a buttered 1 quart casserole and bake in a 375 degree oven for 30-40 minutes, or until a knife inserted in the center comes out clean.
4 servings.

APRICOT SWEET POTATO CASSEROLE

1	17-ounce can whole sweet potatoes or 4 medium sweet potatoes, cooked
1	tablespoon frozen orange juice concentrate
2	tablespoons butter, melted
1	tablespoon brown sugar
Salt to taste	
Pinch of nutmeg	
1	egg
½	cup dried apricots, simmered in water 30 minutes, drained and chopped

Mash the sweet potatoes. Mix with the orange juice, butter, sugar, salt and nutmeg. Stir in unbeaten egg and apricot pieces. Spoon into a shallow, buttered casserole. Bake in a 350 degree oven for 30 minutes or until puffed and brown.
4 servings.

234

VEGETABLES

PECAN SWEET POTATO BAKE

1	**2- pound can sweet potatoes or yams**
2	**tablespoons butter**
¼	**teaspoon salt**
5-6	**tablespoons half and half**

PECAN SAUCE:

1	**cup brown sugar**
2	**tablespoons butter**
1	**teaspoon vanilla extract**
⅓	**cup half and half**
1	**cup pecans**

Heat the sweet potatoes in their juice. Remove from heat and drain; add butter and salt. Using an electric mixer, mash the sweet potatoes with the half and half until light and fluffy. Spread into a buttered 9" or 10" deep dish pie pan.

To make the sauce, combine brown sugar, butter, vanilla, and half and half in saucepan. Heat to boiling, stirring occasionally. Boil 2-3 minutes. Pour sauce over sweet potatoes. Top with pecans and bake in a 350 degree oven for 20-30 minutes.
6-8 servings.

SWEET POTATO CHIPS

3	**medium sweet potatoes**
1	**tablespoon salt**
2	**teaspoons sugar**
1	**teaspoon cinnamon**
Vegetable oil for frying	

Peel the sweet potatoes and cut into ⅛" slices. Place the slices in a bowl and cover with cold water. Stir in the salt. Let stand for 10 minutes. Heat ¼" of oil in a pan until hot, but not smoking, 360-370 degrees. Drain the potatoes and pat dry. Fry a few slices at a time until lightly browned, about 3 minutes per side. Drain on paper towels and sprinkle with a mixture of the sugar and cinnamon. Keep warm in the oven while frying the remaining slices.
4-6 servings.

SPINACH SOUTHWORTH

½	pound fresh mushrooms
8	tablespoons butter, divided
3	10-ounce packages frozen chopped spinach, thawed
11	ounces cream cheese, room temperature

Juice of 1 lemon

Seasoned salt and pepper to taste

Dash of nutmeg

2	14-ounce cans artichoke hearts

Remove mushroom caps, leaving them whole; slice stems. Brown caps and stems in 3 tablespoons butter. Set caps aside for top of the casserole. Drain the spinach and squeeze out excess liquid. Soften cream cheese and blend with 5 tablespoons of melted butter, stirring until smooth. Add the lemon juice, mushroom stems and spinach to the cheese mixture. Stir in seasoned salt, pepper and nutmeg; blend well. Cut artichoke hearts in half and place in a buttered 9" x 13" baking dish. Spoon spinach mixture over artichokes. Arrange reserved mushroom caps on top. Cover with foil. Punch several holes in foil and bake in a 350 degree oven for 30 minutes or until well heated. Dish may be prepared ahead and refrigerated; increase cooking time slightly.
8-10 servings.

SKILLET SPINACH

1	pound fresh spinach, washed, stemmed and drained
2	tablespoons butter
4	tablespoons olive oil
4	tablespoons prosciutto, chopped
2	tablespoons fresh garlic, minced

Combine butter and olive oil in a large skillet. Heat until butter melts and add prosciutto and garlic. Sauté briefly. Add spinach and cook, stirring constantly, until spinach is wilted and excess water has evaporated.
4 servings.

VEGETABLES

CORN SOUFFLÉ TOMATOES

8	**medium tomatoes**
Salt and pepper to taste	
2	**eggs, room temperature**
2	**tablespoons flour**
2	**tablespoons sugar**
½	**teaspoon baking powder**
1	**cup cream**
1	**cup fresh corn kernels**
2	**tablespoons margarine, room temperature**
Chopped parsley	
3-4 slices bacon, cooked crisp, optional	
1	**cup shredded Monterey Jack cheese, optional**

Cut tops off the tomatoes, scoop out insides, sprinkle with salt and pepper, and invert onto paper towels to drain. Beat eggs in a medium bowl. Mix in flour, sugar, baking powder, cream, corn and margarine. If desired, add crumbled bacon or Monterey Jack cheese. Spoon mixture into tomato shells. Place in greased muffin tins and bake in a 350 degree oven until custard is puffed, lightly browned and firm to the touch, 45 minutes. 8 servings.

ZUCCHINI PUFF

6	**cups zucchini, cut into ¼″ thick slices**
3	**cups boiling water**
3	**large eggs**
1½	**cups mayonnaise**
½	**cup green pepper, chopped**
¾	**cup Parmesan cheese, grated**
¾	**cup sharp Cheddar cheese, shredded**
1½	**medium onions, chopped**
Salt and pepper to taste ·	

Blanch zucchini 3-4 minutes in boiling water; rinse in cold water to stop cooking. Drain well; set aside. Beat eggs until frothy and stir in mayonnaise, green pepper, Parmesan, Cheddar, onions, salt and pepper. Add zucchini and blend well. Turn into a buttered 8″ x 10″ baking pan and bake in a 350 degree oven for 40-45 minutes. Puff is done when a knife inserted in the center comes out clean. Let rest a few minutes before cutting into squares to serve. 8 servings.

STUFFED ZUCCHINI

3	medium zucchini
1	10 ounce package frozen spinach, thawed and squeezed dry
2	cloves garlic, minced
½	cup onion, chopped
1	tablespoon parsley, snipped
¼	cup dry Italian bread crumbs
Pinch each, oregano, marjaram and thyme	
2	eggs, beaten
½	cup Parmesan cheese, grated
Salt and pepper to taste	
Olive oil	

Cut zucchini in half lengthwise, remove and discard center. Set aside. Mix together, in a bowl, the spinach, onion, garlic, parsley, bread crumbs and the seasonings. Add the beaten eggs and mix thoroughly. Stuff the zucchini shells with the spinach mixture. Oil an ovenproof pan large enough to hold the zucchini shells. Sprinkle shells with grated Parmesan. Cover loosely with foil and bake in a 350 degree oven 30-35 minutes.
Serves 3-4.

VEGETABLE MEDLEY SAUCE

½	cup mayonnaise
½	cup sour cream
1	teaspoon white Worcestershire sauce
¼	teaspoon salt
Pepper to taste	
½	cup Cheddar cheese, shredded
½	cup green onions, chopped

Combine mayonnaise, sour cream, Worcestershire sauce, salt and pepper. In separate bowl, combine cheese and green onions. Add mayonnaise mixture to cheese mixture and mix well. Pour over medley of vegetables and bake in 350 degree oven 3 minutes or microwave on high 1½ minutes.

DESSERTS

DESSERTS

MICHIGAN APPLE DUMPLINGS

12	medium apples
3	cups flour
2	teaspoons baking powder
1	teaspoon salt
1	cup vegetable shortening
¾	cup milk
2	teaspoons brown sugar
½	teaspoon cinnamon
¼	cup butter
1½	cups sugar
2	cups water
½	teaspoon cinnamon
4	tablespoons margarine

Peel and core apples. Mix flour, baking powder and salt. Cut in shortening; gradually add milk. Stir until dough is soft. Roll dough into rectangle; cut into 7" squares.

Put apples on top of 7" squares. Moisten edge of dough with water and bring each corner up over apple. Mix brown sugar and cinnamon together; fill apple core with mixture and dot with butter. Pinch to seal dough on top of apple. Place sugar, water, cinnamon and margarine in a saucepan and bring to a boil. Put apples in baking pan, pour hot sauce over apples. Bake in 400 degree oven 40 minutes, basting after 20 minutes. Serves 12.

BAKED HAZELNUT PEARS

2	Bosc pears, peeled, halved lengthwise and cored
¼	cup hazelnut liqueur
2	tablespoons unsalted butter, softened
2	tablespoons sugar
¼	cup heavy cream
½-1	ounce semisweet chocolate, melted and slightly cooled

Arrange pears cut side down in a shallow baking dish just large enough to hold them in a single layer. Pour liqueur over pears and dot with butter. Sprinkle with sugar and bake in a 425 degree oven for 30 minutes, basting occasionally. Pears should be tender. Swirl the cream into the dish and cook 5 minutes more. Remove the pears to 4 dessert bowls and stir the sauce to blend. Pour sauce over pears and top with a small dollop of chocolate.
4 servings.

GRAPES FLORENTINE

1½	pounds seedless grapes
3	egg yolks
⅔	cup sugar
⅔	cup dry sherry
1	cup heavy cream, whipped

Rinse and drain grapes. Remove stems and chill. In the top of a double boiler over simmering water, beat egg yolks until thick and pale yellow. Gradually beat in sugar. Stir in sherry and cook, stirring, until slightly thickened. Refrigerate overnight or until cold and set. When ready to serve, fold whipped cream into egg mixture. Put grapes into stemmed glasses and spoon sauce over the top.
6-8 servings.

GREEN GRAPES IN COGNAC

3	pounds fresh seedless grapes
¾	cup honey
¾	cup cognac
1	tablespoon fresh lemon juice
1-2 cups sour cream	

Wash grapes and drain thoroughly. Remove stems. Combine honey, cognac and lemon juice and toss with the grapes. Refrigerate for 5 hours, stirring occasionally. Serve in chilled sherbet dishes, topped with sour cream.
8-10 servings.

EDIBLE WATER LILIES

½ pound white confectioners coating or almond bark

Red food coloring

⅛ teaspoon mint extract

⅛ teaspoon almond extract

6 4″ round balloons

6 spring clips

Add coating or bark to the top of a double boiler and place over hot water, stirring to melt. Remove 3 tablespoons melted coating to another container and into this stir 1 drop each of red food coloring and mint extract. Stir almond extract into remaining white coating. Inflate each balloon, twist top and secure with a clip — do not tie into a knot.

Pour white chocolate coating onto sheet of foil or parchment paper. Drizzle pink chocolate over the white. Roll bottom of each balloon in pink chocolate rocking back and form and rotating bottom to form petals. Make sure coating is thick. Stand each balloon on a foil or parchment lined sheet. Chill in the refrigerator until cold to the touch and solidified. To remove the balloon, hold the opening with one hand, and remove the clip, slowly letting out the air in the balloon.

Serve chocolate cups filled with ice cream, mousse, fruit or candy. Makes 6 cups.

See photo illustration.

CHOCOLATE CREAM SUPREME

½	cup butter
2	cups confectioners' sugar
3	eggs, separated
½	teaspoon salt
½	teaspoon vanilla
2	squares unsweetened chocolate, melted
2	cups vanilla wafer crumbs, divided
1	quart vanilla ice cream

Cream together the butter and sugar; beat in egg yolks. Add salt, vanilla and melted chocolate, mixing well. Beat egg whites until stiff and fold into chocolate mixture. Butter 2 freezer trays and sprinkle in 1½ cups vanilla wafer crumbs. Spread chocolate mixture evenly into the 2 trays and freeze until firm. Soften ice cream and spread over frozen chocolate mixture. Top with remaining ½ cup crumbs and refreeze.
8 servings.

EASY CHOCOLATE MOUSSE

2	egg yolks
12	ounces semisweet chocolate chips
1	cup scalded milk
½	teaspoon instant coffee
2	tablespoons brandy, optional
4	egg whites
½	cup sugar

Put the egg yolks, chocolate chips, milk, coffee and brandy in a blender. Blend on high speed just long enough to liquify the chips. In a separate bowl, beat the egg whites until frothy. Slowly add the sugar and beat until stiff. Fold into the chocolate mixture. Pour mousse into a serving bowl or into individual dishes and refrigerate.
10-12 servings.

DESSERTS

WILL NOT LAST SUGAR COOKIES

1 **cup sugar**
1 **cup margarine**
1½ **cups white flour**
½ **teaspoon vinegar**
½ **teaspoon soda**

Cream together sugar and margarine. Add flour, vinegar and soda. Form dough into balls using about 1 teaspoon each. Press thin with the bottom of a glass that has been greased and dipped in sugar. Bake in preheated 325 degree oven on ungreased cookie sheets for 9-10 minutes. Keep in tightly sealed container to retain crispness. Can be frozen. Makes about 4 dozen cookies. Recipe can be doubled.

EASY PEANUT BUTTER COOKIES

1 **cup peanut butter, preferably chunk style**
1 **cup sugar**
1 **egg**
½ **teaspoon vanilla**

Mix peanut butter and sugar, then stir in remaining ingredients. Shape in 1" balls and put on ungreased cookie sheets. Press with fork to flatten slightly. Bake in a preheated 350 degree oven for 12-15 minutes. Cool on racks.

Note: There is no flour in this recipe.
Makes 3 dozen cookies.

POTATO CHIP COOKIES

1	cup butter or margarine
½	cup granulated sugar
1½	teaspoons vanilla
1½	cups all-purpose flour
1	cup potato chips, crushed to crumbs

Cream butter with sugar. Add vanilla and flour. Blend in potato chips. Drop by teaspoonfuls onto greased cookie sheet. Bake in a preheated 375 degree oven for 15 minutes.
Yield: 3 dozen 1"- 1½" cookies.

TOFFEE SQUARES

25	saltines
1	cup brown sugar
1	cup margarine or butter
1	12-ounce package chocolate chips
½	cup chopped nuts

Preheat oven to 450 degrees. Grease a 9" x 13" baking pan. Line the bottom with crackers. Combine sugar and margarine in saucepan. Cook slowly over low heat for 8 minutes, stirring occasionally. Pour over crackers and bake for 8 minutes. Remove from oven and sprinkle with chocolate pieces. When chocolate is soft, spread evenly over top. Sprinkle with nuts. Cool 2 minutes and cut between crackers to allow chocolate to ooze between cookies. When partially cooled, remove cookies to waxed paper and cool. Cut each cracker in half.
Yield: Around 4 dozen.

WHOOPIE PIES

1	cup vegetable shortening
2	cups sugar
2	whole eggs and 2 egg yolks (reserve whites for filling)
1	cup sour milk or buttermilk
4	cups all-purpose flour
1	cup cocoa
½	teaspoon salt
1	teaspoon baking soda
1½	teaspoons baking powder
1	cup hot water

FILLING:

2	egg whites
2	teaspoons vanilla
4	teaspoons flour
2	teaspoons confectioners sugar
2	teaspoons milk
1½	cups vegetable shortening
1	pound confectioners sugar

Cream shortening and sugar in a large bowl. Beat in the 2 eggs and 2 egg yolks and sour milk. Combine flour, cocoa, salt, baking soda and baking powder and add to above mixture. Stir in water.

Drop by rounded tablespoonfuls onto a greased cookie sheet. Bake in preheated 375 degree oven for 10 minutes. Cool completely on wire rack.

Prepare filling while cookies are cooling. Mix egg whites, vanilla, flour, 2 teaspoons confectioners sugar, milk and shortening. Beat in the 1 pound of sugar.

When cookies are cool, place a generous amount of filling between two cookies.
Makes about 3 dozen filled cookies.

OATMEAL COCONUT COOKIES

1	cup butter or margarine
1	cup brown sugar
½	cup granulated sugar
2	eggs
1	teaspoon vanilla
1½	cups all-purpose flour
1	teaspoon baking powder
1	teaspoon baking soda
1	teaspoon salt
2	cups oven-toasted rice cereal
½	cup chopped nuts
2	cups dry oatmeal
2	cups coconut, flaked or shredded

Cream butter, sugars, and eggs; add vanilla. Blend in flour, baking powder, soda, and salt. Add cereal, nuts, oatmeal and coconut and mix well. Drop by tablespoonfuls on a lightly-greased baking sheet. Flatten cookies with fork and leave space between them. Bake 10-12 minutes until golden brown in a preheated 350 degree oven. Yield: About 4½ dozen.

BROWNIES, DRUNK OR SOBER

½	cup margarine
4	1-ounce squares unsweetened chocolate
1½	cups sugar
3	eggs
¾	cup all-purpose flour
¾	teaspoon baking powder
½	teaspoon salt
1	teaspoon vanilla
1	cup walnuts, chopped
¼	cup bourbon whiskey, if desired

Melt margarine and chocolate together over hot water, or in microwave. Set aside to cool. In 1-quart mixing bowl, beat eggs until light yellow. Add sugar, then the chocolate mixture. Stir in flour, baking powder and salt, mixing just until blended. Add nuts and vanilla. Pour batter into greased and floured 7" x 11" pan. Bake at 350 degrees for 30 minutes. That's the sober version. To bake drunken brownies — pour ¼ cup bourbon over warm brownies after removing from oven. Frost the bars, if desired. Yield: About 20 bars.

MINCEMEAT BARS

FILLING:

1½ cups mincemeat (prepared —
     available in glass jars)

¼   cup sugar

1   tablespoon cornstarch

½   teaspoon lemon juice

Cook over low heat, stirring until thick. Make before mixing crumb mixture.

1½ cups sifted flour

1   teaspoon baking soda

½   teaspoon salt

2½ cups uncooked quick-cooking
     oatmeal (not instant)

1½ cups light brown sugar,
     packed

½   cup walnuts, chopped
     medium fine

1   cup melted margarine

Combine flour, soda, salt, oatmeal, sugar and walnuts. Add melted margarine and mix well. Press half of mixture into a greased 12" x 8" cake pan. Spread with mincemeat filling; cover with remaining half of oatmeal mixture and press down. Bake for 30 minutes in a preheated 350 degree oven.
Makes 48 bars.

APRICOT - ALMOND SQUARES

CRUST:

1	cup + 2 tablespoons flour
⅓	cup + 1 tablespoon sugar
½	egg
½	cup softened butter or margarine

FILLING:

⅓	cup almond paste
1	egg
2	teaspoons milk
¼	cup + 1 tablespoon sugar

TOP:

4	tablespoons apricot preserves
1	teaspoon water

GLAZE:

¼	cup confectioners sugar, thinned with a little lemon juice

Mix all crust ingredients together. Pat ⅔ of dough into bottom of an 8" square pan. Mix all filling ingredients together. Spread over crust in pan.

Roll remaining ⅓ of dough to a ¼" thickness. Cut into strips and arrange in a lattice pattern over filling. Bake in a preheated 300 degree oven for 50-60 minutes, or until golden brown. While cake is still warm, spread apricot preserve mixture over top. Drizzle with glaze when cool. Cut into squares. Makes 20 bars.

CANTERBURY PIE

2	eggs
1	teaspoon salt
1	cup sugar
¾	cup currants
½	cup chopped walnuts
½	cup chopped dates
1	teaspoon vanilla
½	cup melted butter
1	unbaked pie shell

Beat together eggs and salt. Gradually beat in sugar. Stir in remaining ingredients and pour into pie shell. Bake in a preheated 350 degree oven for 30 minutes.

JAPANESE FRUIT PIE

6	tablespoons margarine
1	cup sugar
3	eggs
1	teaspoon vinegar
½	cup coconut
½	cup chopped nuts
½	cup raisins
1	unbaked pie shell

Cream sugar and margarine. Add eggs and beat well. Stir in vinegar, coconut, nuts and raisins. Pour into pie shell. Preheat oven to 350 degrees. Bake pie on lowest rack for 45-60 minutes, until lightly browned and set.
6 servings.

LEMON PARFAIT PIE

1	9" deep dish pastry crust, baked
½	cup butter or margarine
1	cup sugar
2	tablespoons cornstarch
¼	teaspoon salt
1	tablespoon grated lemon peel
⅓	cup lemon juice
3	eggs, separated
1	quart vanilla ice cream
¼	teaspoon cream of tartar
⅓	cup sugar

Melt butter in the top of a double boiler over simmering water. Stir in sugar, cornstarch and salt. Blend thoroughly. Add lemon peel and juice. Beat egg yolks and stir in until smooth. Continue to cook, stirring constantly, until mixture is thick, 8-10 minutes. Set aside to cool.

Soften 1 pint of the ice cream and spread into the pie shell. Freeze until firm. Spread half of the cooled lemon sauce over the frozen ice cream; return to the freezer until firm. Repeat with the remaining ice cream and sauce, freezing until firm. Beat the egg whites and cream of tartar until soft peaks form. Gradually beat in the sugar. Continue beating until sugar is dissolved and meringue is stiff and glossy. Spread meringue over the pie, being careful to seal meringue to the edge of the pie. Place pie on a baking sheet and cook in a 475 degree oven for 3 minutes or until lightly browned. Return to freezer. 8 servings.

BLOSSOMLAND PEACH PIE

3 cups flour

4 teaspoons sugar

1 teaspoon salt

6 tablespoons unsalted butter, cold, cut into 8 pieces

10 tablespoons lard, cold, cut into 12 pieces

6 tablespoons ice water

5-6 cups peaches, peeled and sliced

GLAZE:

½ cup brown sugar

2 tablespoons flour

⅛ teaspoon salt

¼ cup butter

2 teaspoons lemon juice, or to taste

Place flour, sugar, salt, butter and lard in a food processor fitted with a metal blade and process with several short pulses, until the shortening is the size of peas. Add ice water all at once and process 10 seconds to blend. Turn the pastry onto a floured board. Form into a ball, wrap in plastic wrap and refrigerate 3 hours or overnight. Roll out half of the dough on a floured board. Fit into a lightly greased 9" pie pan. Add sliced peaches. To prepare the glaze, place the brown sugar, flour, salt and butter in a small saucepan and cook gently until thickened. Stir in lemon juice to taste and pour over peaches. Roll out the remaining dough and place over the peaches, or cut into strips for a lattice crust. Brush top with milk, if desired, and sprinkle with cinnamon and sugar. Bake in a preheated 400 degree oven for 45-50 minutes.
6-8 servings.

HEAVENLY ANGEL PIE

4	eggs separated
¼	teaspoon cream of tartar
1	cup superfine sugar
½	cup granulated sugar
3	tablespoons lemon juice
2	teaspoon grated lemon rind
½	pint whipping cream

Beat 4 egg whites until frothy. Add cream of tartar and beat until soft peaks form. Gradually add 1 cup superfine sugar, beating until glossy and mixture stands in firm peaks. Spread on bottom and sides of a buttered 9" pie pan and bake 1 hour in a preheated 250 degree oven. Cool.

While meringue crust is baking, beat the 4 egg yolks until thick and lemon colored. Add ½ cup sugar, lemon juice and rind. Cook in a double boiler over hot water until mixture coats a wooden spoon and is a little thick. It will become more firm as it cools. Set aside to cool.

Whip cream, fold into the cooled custard and pour into the meringue shell. Chill 4 hours or overnight. Can be made ahead. Will not freeze well.

DESSERTS

RUM CRÈME PIE

18 squares graham crackers
⅓ cup sugar
½ cup melted butter
Cinnamon
1 3-ounce package cream cheese
½ cup sugar
2 eggs, beaten
2 tablespoons dark rum
1 cup sour cream
3 tablespoons sugar
1 tablespoon sherry

Combine first four ingredients for crust and pat into 9" pie pan. Mix cream cheese, sugar, eggs and rum. Pour into crust and bake in a preheated oven 375 degrees for 20 minutes. Stir together remaining ingredients and pour over hot filling. Return to oven for 5 minutes. Chill.
Serves 8-16.

APPLE PIZZA PIE

1⅔ cup flour, divided
½ teaspoon salt
½ cup shortening
1 cup sharp Cheddar cheese, shredded
¼ cup ice water
½ cup confectioners sugar
½ cup granulated sugar
½ cup brown sugar
1 teaspoon cinnamon
¼ cup margarine, room temperature
6 cups apples, peeled and sliced
2 tablespoons lemon juice

To make the crust, mix 1⅓ cups flour and salt. Add the shortening and cheese and work until crumbly. Sprinkle in the water and working with a fork, shape the dough into a ball. On a floured surface roll the dough out to fit a 15" pizza pan. Flute the edges. For the filling, mix the sugars, ⅓ cup flour and cinnamon. Sprinkle half the mixture over the crust. Work margarine into the rest of the mixture until crumbly. Arrange the apple slices over the sugar covered dough in overlapping circles. Sprinkle with lemon juice and the remaining sugar mixture. Bake in a preheated 400 degree oven for 30 minutes.

SOUR CREAM APPLE PIE

2	**tablespoons flour**
½	**teaspoon salt**
¾	**cup sugar**
1	**egg, beaten**
1	**cup sour cream**
1	**teaspoon vanilla**
¼	**teaspoon nutmeg**
2	**cups diced, peeled apples**
1	**unbaked 9″ pie shell**

TOPPING:

⅓	**cup sugar**
⅓	**cup flour**
1	**teaspoon cinnamon**
¼	**cup butter or margarine, room temperature**

Sift together flour, salt and sugar. Add egg, sour cream, vanilla and nutmeg, beating until smooth. Stir in apples. Pour into pie shell. Bake in a preheated 350 degree oven for 30 minutes. While pie is baking, prepare topping. Mix all of the ingredients together. Sprinkle over the partially baked pie. Turn the oven up to 400 degrees and continue to bake for 15 minutes, or until browned.
6 servings.

DESSERTS

RASPBERRY BAVARIAN PIE

⅓	cup butter
2½	teaspoons sugar
¼	teaspoon salt
1	egg yolk
1	cup flour
⅓	cup finely chopped almonds
10	ounce package frozen red raspberries, partially thawed and drained
2	egg whites
1	cup sugar
1	tablespoon lemon juice
¼	teaspoon vanilla
¼	teaspoon almond extract
⅛	teaspoon salt
8	ounce tub frozen whipped non-dairy topping, thawed

Preheat oven to 400 degrees; grease a 10" pie plate. Cream butter, sugar and salt until fluffy. Add egg yolk and beat thoroughly. Mix in flour and almonds. Press into prepared pan. Bake 12 minutes, cool.

Place all ingredients for filling, except non-dairy topping, in a large bowl. Beat until mixture thickens and expands in volume, up to 15 minutes. Fold in non-dairy topping. Pile into pastry and freeze at least 8 hours. Wonderful! Can also use 9" x 13" pan or springform pan. Makes 2 pies if you use packaged butter crust.

LEMON THYME CHEESECAKE

2	pounds cream cheese, softened
2	eggs
1	cup sour cream
¾	cup sugar
1	tablespoon finely chopped fresh lemon thyme leaves, or 2 tablespoons dried
1	tablespoon lemon juice
1	teaspoon vanilla
2	tablespoons cornstarch
1	cup graham cracker crumbs
2	tablespoons butter, softened

Lightly beat the eggs with a food processor or mixer. Add the sour cream, sugar, thyme, lemon juice, vanilla and cornstarch. Mix or process until smooth and creamy. Add cream cheese, ½ pound at a time. Mix well. Spread butter on the inside of a 9" springform pan and dust with graham cracker crumbs; shake out any excess crumbs. Pour batter into pan and bake in a preheated 350 degree oven for 55-60 minutes. When cake is done, immediately run a knife around the edge of the pan. Cool on a wire rack 10 minutes, remove sides of pan and cool completely. 10-12 servings.

SMASHING CHOCOLATE TORTE

1	frozen pound cake, thawed
1	6-ounce package semisweet chocolate chips
1	cup sour cream
½	teaspoon instant coffee
1	teaspoon vanilla

Using a serrated knife, cut the cake lengthwise into 6 or 7 layers. In a saucepan over low heat, melt the chocolate chips. Remove from heat and stir in the sour cream, coffee and vanilla. Spread this filling thinly betwen the cake layers. Allow the cake to stand covered in the refrigerator at least 12 hours before slicing.

PUMPKIN TORTE

24	graham crackers, crushed
⅓	cup sugar
½	cup butter or margarine
2	eggs, beaten
¾	cup sugar
8	ounces cream cheese
2	cups pumpkin
3	eggs, separated, reserve whites
½	cup sugar
½	cup milk
½	teaspoon salt
2	teaspoons cinnamon
1	teaspoon nutmeg
1	envelope plain gelatin
¼	cup cold water
¼	cup sugar
½	pint whipping cream, whipped

Mix crushed graham crackers, ⅓ cup sugar and butter; press into 9" x 13" pan. Mix 2 eggs, ¾ cup sugar and cream cheese. Pour over crust and bake at 350 degrees for 20 minutes. Cook pumpkin, egg yolks, ½ cup sugar, milk, salt, cinnamon and nutmeg until mixture thickens. Remove from heat and add gelatin dissolved in cold water. Cool. Beat egg whites with ¼ cup sugar until peaks are formed and fold into pumpkin mixture. Pour over cooled baked crust. Top with whipped cream when cool.
Serves 12-15.

LEMON PUDDING CAKES

2	eggs, separated
¼	cup lemon juice
⅔	cup milk
1	cup sugar
½	cup flour
¼	teaspoon salt

Beat egg whites until stiff; set aside. Beat egg yolks 1 minute. Add lemon juice and milk and beat until smooth. Stir in sugar, flour and salt. Fold into egg whites. Divide the batter among 4 4-ounce individual soufflé dishes, filling to the top. Carefully place the soufflé cups into an 8" x 8" glass baking dish. Pour hot water into the pan around the soufflé cups. Bake in a 350 degree oven for 35-40 minutes. Tops will puff up and may crack. They will collapse a little as they cool. 4 servings.

MICHIGAN PEACH SHORTCAKE

2	cups flour
4	teaspoons baking powder
½	teaspoon salt
½	cup margarine, room temperature
1	12-ounce can evaporated milk, divided
6-8 fresh, ripe peaches, peeled and halved	
1-1½ cups plus 2 tablespoons sugar	
4	eggs

Sift together flour, baking powder and salt. Cut in margarine. Add 1 cup evaporated milk and blend well. Pat mixture into a greased 9" x 13" baking pan. Cover with halved peaches, cut side down. Sprinkle 1-1½ cups sugar over peaches, according to sweetness of peaches. Beat together the eggs, the remaining ½ cup evaporated milk and 2 tablespoons of sugar. Pour over the peaches. Bake in a preheated 400 degree oven for 15 minutes. Reduce heat to 350 degrees and bake for 30 minutes longer. Serve warm, with cream if desired. 8-12 servings.

DESSERTS

MONTMORENCY CHERRY CLAFOUTI

3	**cups pitted fresh sour cherries**
3	**tablespoons Cognac**
1	**tablespoon unsalted butter**
½	**cup sugar**
¾	**cup milk**
¼	**cup heavy cream**
3	**eggs**
1	**teaspoon almond extract**
Pinch of salt	
⅔	**cup all-purpose flour**

Preheat oven to 350 degrees. Combine cherries with Cognac and set aside. Butter a 10" deep dish pie plate or a fluted porcelain tart dish. Dust the bottom with 1 teaspoon sugar. In a blender combine the milk, cream, eggs, remaining sugar, almond extract, salt, and flour. Blend at high speed for 1 minute. Pour ½ cup batter into the dish. Arrange cherries over batter in an even layer, drizzle with the Cognac. Pour the remaining batter over the cherries. Bake for 45-60 minutes, or until top is puffed and golden brown and the batter is set. Serves 6-8.

MEXICAN CHOCOLATE CAKE

1	**18.5-ounce package devil's food cake mix**
4	**eggs**
1	**cup sour cream**
1	**cup coffee-flavored liqueur**
¾	**cup vegetable oil**
1	**cup semisweet chocolate chips**

In a large bowl combine cake mix, eggs, sour cream, liqueur and vegetable oil. Beat with an electric mixer on low speed until blended. Beat 3-5 minutes on medium speed. Stir in chocolate chips. Pour into a greased and floured 10" bundt pan. Bake in a preheated 350 degree oven for 55-60 minutes. Cool in the pan for 30 minutes. Loosen and invert onto a rack to cool completely. This very rich cake needs no frosting, but may be served with whipped cream. 12-15 servings.

PIÑA COLADA CAKE

1   18-ounce package white cake mix

1   3⅝-ounce package instant chocolate pudding mix

4   eggs

⅓   cup rum

¼   cup oil

½   cup water

FROSTING:

1   8-ounce can crushed pineapple, undrained

1   3⅝-ounce package instant coconut cream pudding mix

⅓   cup rum

1   9-ounce container non-dairy whipped topping

To make the cake, combine the first 6 ingredients in a large bowl and beat on medium speed for 4 minutes. Pour batter into 2 greased and floured 9" round cake pans. Bake in a preheated 350 degree oven for 25-30 minutes. Cool in pans for several minutes; invert onto a wire rack and cool completely. To make the frosting, combine the pineapple, coconut pudding mix, and rum, blending well. Fold in the whipped topping. Spread between the layers and over the top and sides. Garnish with coconut, if desired.
12 servings.

FIVE DAY CAKE

2	cups sour cream
2	cups sugar
4	ounces flaked coconut
9	ounces non-dairy whipped topping
1	package yellow cake mix with pudding
Additional coconut for garnish	

Mix sour cream, sugar and coconut. Cover and refrigerate overnight. The next day make the cake following package directions, but baking in 3 8" cake pans. After cooling, split each layer in half to make 6 layers. Set aside 1 cup of the sour cream mixture and use the rest to fill between the cake layers. Mix the whipped topping with the reserved sour cream mixture and spread over the cake. Sprinkle with additional coconut, if desired. Cover cake and refrigerate for 2-5 days before serving. Cake will keep, covered, in the refrigerator for up to 2 weeks.
12-15 servings.

MANDARIN ORANGE CAKE

1	cup sugar
1	cup flour
1	egg
1	teaspoon baking soda
¼	teaspoon salt
1	11-ounce can mandarin oranges, drained

TOPPING:

¾	cup sugar
3	tablespoons unsalted butter
3	tablespoons milk
½	cup chopped walnuts

Mix all of the cake ingredients together in a bowl with an electric mixer. Pour into a greased 8" x 8" cake pan and bake in a preheated 350 degree oven for 40 minutes. To make the topping, put all the topping ingredients into a small saucepan and bring to a boil. Pour over the warm cake and place under the broiler for 1 minute.
6 servings.

DUTCH ALMOND BUTTER CAKE

1	egg, beaten
1½	cups sugar
1	cup almond paste, canned or fresh
1	cup butter, softened
2	cups flour

Mix egg and sugar. Stir in almond paste. Add butter and mix well. Blend in the flour. This dough is stiff and is best mixed with the hands. When dough is well combined, pat into a greased 9" round or square pan. Bake in a preheated 350 degree oven for 35 minutes.
Serves 8-10.

CHOCOLATE MOUSSE CAKE

4	4-ounce bars German sweet chocolate
3	tablespoons water
3	tablespoons Amaretto
4	egg yolks
4	tablespoons confectioners sugar
4	eggs whites, stiffly beaten
2	cups heavy cream, whipped
2	4-ounce packages lady fingers

Break chocolate into pieces and melt in top of a double boiler over hot water. Add water and Amaretto, blending with electric mixer on low. Remove pan from hot water and add egg yolks, one at a time, beating after each addition. Add sugar and mix well. Fold in stiffly beaten egg whites, then fold in whipped cream. Line the sides and bottom of a 9" springform pan with some of the lady fingers. Pour chocolate mixture into pan and arrange the remaining lady fingers on top. Cover with plastic wrap and chill for 12-24 hours. Remove ring and serve with additional whipped cream, if desired.
12 servings.

DESSERTS

CHOCOLATE SOUFFLÉ CAKE WITH GRAND MARNIER CRÈME

6	ounces semisweet chocolate
2	tablespoons water
8	eggs, separated
¾	cup sugar
6	ounces unsalted butter at room temperautre
¾	cup flour, sifted

GRAND MARNIER CRÈME

5	egg yolks
½	cup sugar
1½	tablespoons cornstarch
1	tablespoon Grand Marnier liqueur
1½	cups heavy cream

Cake: Combine chocolate and water in top of double boiler. Place over hot water until chocolate melts. Let chocolate cool until warm. Cream together egg yolks with sugar until thick enough to form a ribbon when tipped from a spoon. Fold in warm chocolate and softened butter. Fold in flour just until it is all incorporated. Beat egg whites until stiff but not dry. Gently fold whites into chocolate mixture. Pour batter into greased and lightly sugared 8" springform pan. Bake in a preheated 350 degree oven about 1 hour, or until wooden pick inserted in center comes out clean. Cool at room temperature away from drafts.

Grand Marnier Crème: Cream together egg yolks and sugar until mixture is thick enough to form a ribbon when tipped from a spoon. Add cornstarch and Grand Marnier. Continue mixing at lowest speed just until all ingredients are well blended. Scald cream. Transfer yolk mixture to the top of a double boiler over simmering water. Gradually add scalded cream. Cook about 20 minutes or until thick.

To serve, cover bottoms of dessert plates with a thin layer of Grand Marnier Crème. Place a wedge of cake at room temperature in center of cold crème.
Serves 12-16.

PINEAPPLE CAKE

2   cups cake flour

1⅓ cups sugar

2½ teaspoons baking powder

½   teaspoon salt

½   cup vegetable shortening,
     room temperature

1   cup less 2 tablespoons milk

½   teaspoon vanilla

2   eggs

PINEAPPLE FILLING:

1   20-ounce can unsweetened
     crushed pineapple, undrained

2   level tablespoons cornstarch

SEVEN MINUTE ICING:

1   cup sugar

2   egg whites

3   tablespoons water

¼   teaspoon cream of tartar

Pinch of salt

½   teaspoon vanilla

To make the cake, combine the flour, sugar, baking powder, salt and shortening. Mix the milk and vanilla and add to the dry ingredients; beat 3 minutes. Add the eggs and beat 2 minutes. Pour into a greased and floured 9" x 13" baking pan. Bake in a preheated 350 degree oven 20-25 minutes. Cool completely.

To make the filling, combine the pineapple and cornstarch in a small saucepan and cook, stirring, over low heat until thickened. Cool filling and spread over cake.

To make the icing, combine the sugar, egg whites, water, cream of tartar and salt in the top of a double boiler over hot water. Cook, beating constantly, until stiff peaks form, 5-7 minutes; beat in vanilla. Spread frosting over pineapple filling.
15-20 servings.

WATERMELON SLICE SORBET

4	**kiwi fruits, peeled and cut into chunks**
⅔	**cup sugar, divided**
4	**cups watermelon, seeded and cubed**
⅓	**cup cranberry juice**

Place kiwi fruit and ⅓ cup sugar in a food processor fitted with a metal blade. Process until smooth and sugar is dissolved. Transfer to a shallow pan and freeze until almost firm. Process again until smooth. Line a 1 quart bowl with plastic wrap and pour in kiwi mixture. Cover the exterior of a smaller bowl (one that will fit inside the larger bowl) with plastic wrap. Press the smaller bowl into the larger one so that the sorbet fills the gap between the two bowls. Freeze until firm.

While the kiwi layer is freezing, make the watermelon layer. Combine the watermelon, cranberry juice and remaining sugar in a food processor and process until smooth and sugar is dissolved. Transfer to a shallow pan and freeze until almost firm. Process again until smooth. Take kiwi mixture out of the freezer and remove the small bowl. Pour the watermelon mixture over the kiwi layer. Freeze until firm. Unmold onto serving plate and cut into slices. Garnish with fresh mint, if desired.

6-8 servings.

See photo illustration.

MINT SHERBET

1	envelope unflavored gelatin
2	cups sugar
1	cup firmly packed fresh mint leaves, chopped
1¾	cups pineapple juice
¼	cup fresh lemon juice
2	tablespoons grated lemon rind
2	egg whites

Soften gelatin in ½ cup cold water. In a saucepan combine sugar with 2 cups of water and boil for 3 minutes. Pour hot liquid over gelatin, stirring until dissolved. Add mint leaves, cover and let stand 1½ hours, stirring occasionally. Strain liquid and add pineapple juice, lemon juice and lemon rind. Pour into a shallow metal pan and freeze until firm, 3-4 hours. Scoop frozen mixture into a bowl and beat until fluffy. Beat the egg whites until stiff and fold into the frozen mixture. Return to freezer until ready to serve.

Note: Add a few drops of green food coloring when folding in the egg whites for a more colorful dessert.

ORANGE ICE

1½	cups bittersweet orange marmalade
¼	cup fresh lime juice
3	cups apricot nectar
½	cup fresh orange juice

Mix all of the ingredients together in a microwave proof container. Microwave on HIGH power for 6 to 8 minutes. Strain. Freeze in an ice-cream maker according to manufacturer's directions.

Yield 1 quart. Serve with Blueberry Sauce.

STRAWBERRY SORBET

4	**cups fresh ripe strawberries, hulled, wiped**
2	**cups sugar syrup, directions follow**

Juice of ½ orange

Juice of ½ lemon

To Garnish:

Fresh strawberries, if desired

Mint leaves or edible leaves, if desired

SUGAR SYRUP:

2	**pounds superfine sugar**
4	**cups water**

In a food processor/blender, process strawberries and ½ of sugar syrup to a smooth purée. Mix in remaining syrup and orange and lemon juice. Pour into several undivided ice trays. Cover. Place in freezer; freeze to a slush. Return to food processor/blender. Process until light and smooth. Return to trays; re-cover; freeze until firm. Garnish with strawberries and mint leaves or edible leaves, if desired. Makes 6 to 8 servings.

In a large saucepan bring sugar and water to a gentle boil. Reduce heat until bubbles break surface. Simmer 10 minutes. Remove from heat; cool before using or storing. When cooled, syrup can be refrigerated in a covered glass or plastic container for 2 to 3 weeks. This amount is sufficient for at least 4 recipes.

BLUEBERRY SAUCE

3	**cups fresh blueberries**
½	**cup sugar**
1½	**teaspoons cinnamon**
½	**teaspoon freshly grated nutmeg**

Combine all ingredients in a heavy bottom saucepan. Cook for 10 minutes over low heat, stirring frequently. Serve warm or cold. Yield 3 cups.

EASY RICH FUDGE SAUCE

3	**1-ounce squares unsweetened chocolate, chopped**
¼	**cup butter or margarine**
1½	**cups confectioners sugar**
1	**5¾-ounce can evaporated milk**
⅛	**teaspoon salt**
½	**teaspoon vanilla**

In the top of a double boiler over barely simmering water, combine chocolate, butter, sugar, evaporated milk and salt. Cook, stirring constantly, until chocolate has melted and sauce has thickened, about 15 minutes. Stir in vanilla.

ORANGE RUM SAUCE

1	**cup freshly squeezed orange juice**
½	**cup sugar**
½	**cup water**
1	**teaspoon cornstarch**
Dash salt	
¼	**cup rum**
1	**teaspoon grated orange rind**

In the top of a double boiler combine orange juice, sugar, water, cornstarch and salt. Cook over simmering water until thickened. Add rum and orange peel, stirring to blend. Chill sauce before serving over ice cream or cake.

COCONUT PEAKS

½	cup butter
3	cups shredded coconut
2	cups confectioners sugar
6	ounces semi-sweet chocolate, melted

Melt butter, remove from heat and stir in coconut and confectioners sugar. Shape into balls about the size of a large walnut. Dip bottom of each ball into melted chocolate and place on waxed paper. Chill until firm and serve chilled.

ENGLISH TOFFEE

1	cup sugar
1	cup butter (do not use margarine)
3	tablespoons water
1	cup chopped nuts
½	pound chocolate bar
1½	teaspoons vanilla

Combine sugar, butter and water over heat, stirring constantly until mixture reaches hard crack stage — 300 degrees. Add vanilla and half the nuts; then pour out on a cookie sheet. While still hot, place chocolate bar on top and spread evenly. Sprinkle with remainder of nuts. When cold, break into pieces. Makes 1¼ pounds.

NUT GOODIES

1	12-ounce package chocolate chips
1	12-ounce package butterscotch chips
2	cups smooth peanut butter
2	cups salted peanuts, no skins
1	cup butter or margarine
½	cup evaporated milk
¼	cup dry regular vanilla pudding
2	pounds confectioners sugar
1½	teaspoons maple flavoring

In the top of a double boiler, melt the chips and peanut butter. Pour half of the mixture into an oiled 13" x 15" pan and refrigerate. Add peanuts to the remaining mixture and keep in double boiler.

In a medium saucepan combine butter, milk and pudding; mix and cook 1 minute; pour over confectioners sugar and beat until smooth. Beat in flavoring. Spread over chilled layer and top with remaining peanut mixture. Refrigerate until set. Cut into squares. Store in refrigerator or freezer.

PRALINES

1	cup brown sugar
1	cup white sugar
⅔	cup evaporated milk
½	teaspoon vanilla
1½	cups whole pecans

In a medium saucepan mix the two sugars and milk thoroughly. Cook over moderate heat stirring constantly to the soft boil stage — 238 degrees-240 degrees on candy thermometer. Cool slightly. Beat for 1 minute or until glossy. Mix in vanilla and pecans. Drop by tablespoon onto a buttered wax paper. If too thick, thin with drops of water.
Makes 18-24 candies.

INDEX

273

INDEX

INDEX

INDEX

INDEX

INDEX

INDEX

INDEX

INDEX

281

INDEX

INDEX

INDEX

RECIPE CONTRIBUTORS

The Committee would like to thank the following people for submitting recipes and for providing assistance in testing. We hope no names have been omitted.

Shirley Abbott
Charlotte Alberts
Barbara Aldrich
Jane Ammeson
Dawn Ankli
Barbara Arnt
Ryan Arnt
Gray Atkinson
Georgia Atwood
Marion Avery
Norma Baker
Annabelle Bankston
Yvonne Barlow
Pearl Batt
Sam Batt
Cay Beckmann
Suzanne Beckmann
Marilyn Beemer
Bud Benning
Margaret Bensinger
Peg Bentley
Elnora Berk
Ruth Berliner
Celina Lin Bevelhymer
Betty Bingham
Jan Bishop
Georgia Boerma
Esther Boonstra
Bette Boothby
Kathryn Borland
Susan Borland
Joan V. Born
Georgia Bradley
Kye Brinkman
Shirley Broihier
Edalene Brown
Katherine Brown
Maxine Brule
Mary C. Buesing
Patricia Burr
Barbara Butler
June Caldwell
Mickey Campbell
Kate Chappell

Billie Child
Bob Christiano
Lynne Christiano
Nancy Clark
Mary M. Coleman
Alice Collins
Georgiana Conrad
Sherry Conybeare
Maria Cook
Jean Coon
Eugenie Cooper
Barbara Crow
Alice Crowell
Shirley Curry
Elaine Curtis
Irene Cutler
Marian Danielson
Phyllis Danielson
Irmgard (Kim) Davis
Mary Dey
Barbara Dove
Inez Dumke
Mary Lou Duncan
Barbara Eddinger
Irene Edinger
Lucy Eisele
Arlene Emery
Mary Eppelheimer
Marion Evans
Wilma Evans
Millie Feather
Carol Filstrup
Jan Fischer
Elaine Flamm
Vickie Florin
Lorraine Foertsch
Carolyn Frank
Fay Freridge
Florence Gast
Lou Gast
Mary Gates
Carol Geldhof
Joan Gersonde
Gloria Gioseffi

Joan Gleiss
Barbara Globensky
Karna Globensky
Grace Goodman
Phyllis Goulet
Sarabel Goulet
Helen Battin Gray
Kathryn A. Greene
Judy Greenwood
Richard Greenwood
Wendy Greenwood
Linda Griswold
Bev Gross
Dottie Grumbine
Klee Grumbine
Hedy Hagen
Barbara Hall
Cynthia Hall
Shirley Hanley
Mary Lou Hanson
Diana Harper
Pat Heaps
Heather Hellwig
Janet Helsley
Jeanie Heltzel
Carol Jo Hemingway
Barbara Henderson
Madalyn Higgins
Margaret Hills
Kris Hosbein
Joyce Howell
Emily Hrach
Joan Humphrey
Mary E. Hunter
Esther Jacobs
Ginny Jaeger
Nancy J. Johns
Genevieve Jones
Diana Kamp
Judy Kauffman
Linda Ketterer
Rosie Kiley
Eva Kinney
Judy Kinney

RECIPE CONTRIBUTORS (continued)

Helen Kirchoff
Jean Kirk
Carol Klassen
Dottie Klett
Sherry Kniola
Al Kochka
Olga Krasl
Anne Kreiger
Barbra Kruggel
Carol Ladrow
Mary Ann Lagoni
Martha Lateulere
Marilyn Laurin
Sybil Levin
Lois F. Lewis
Sylvia Lieberg
Lisa Lieberg-Stahl
Eleanor Liskey
Ruth Lovell
Marcia Lundeen
Marianne Maley
Gary Manigold
Nancy Marchese
Nancy Mathieu
Barbara Maynard
Peggy McAllister
Helen McDonell
Caryl Meister
Susan Meny
Georgia Merchant
Mary Mielke
Dorothy Miller
Mary Elizabeth Miller
Phyllis Miller
Joyce Miskill
Glenda Monteith
Phyllis Montgomery
Gloria Muth
Jeanne Nagle
Roger Newmann
Shirley Nieb
Sue Nolin
Edna Norris
Jan Ogonowski
Cindy Salvino Ojczyk
J. Charles Ojczyk
Pam Olson
Milly Ott

Ann Palenske
Joann Palmer
Margie Pannell
Doris Parr
Virginia Pearson
Ann Perkins
Jeanne Pettegrew
Jackie Pheeney
Bonnie Phillips
Margie Piraino
Peggy Platts
Joy Powley
Esther Radom
Judy Randall
Ellen Rasbach
Rosalyn Reeder
Ruth Rhode
Betts Rittmeyer
Tara Robinson
Margaret Rohn
Loie Rokely
Dorothy Rollert
Viola Ross
Rose Marie Roth
Lynda Roti
Claire Ruspino
Lela Russell
Anna Ruth
Gwenn Schadler
Ruth Schafer
Marge Schilling
Daniella Schott
Bertha Schroeder
Anita Schultz
Ardys Schultz
Dorothy Schwerdt
Jan Sharon
Connie Shaw
Mickie Shipman
Debra Silverthorn
Hilda Sinclair
May Sisson
Patti R. Sizer
Jean Skinner
Mary Elizabeth Small
Jan Sonneman
Peg Southworth
Fredda Sparks
Sue Spitler

Jean Stark
Beatrice Starke
Carol Starks
Dorothy Steele-Gephart
Sylvia Stellwagen
Norma Stephen
Keith Stevens
Kathy Strunk-VanDerHulst
Dee Sykora
Dorothy Symons
Beverly Thompson
Jeanne Tibbitts
Marion Tiffany
Phyllis Tincher
Doris Tippett
Marcia Troff
Barbara Troost
Thelma Troost
Amey R. Upton
Fred S. Upton
Pearl Urist
Vera Van Antwerp
Elaine Vanderberg
Phyllis Van Osdal
Louis Voges
Sandra Voges
Delores Wade
Mary Jo Walsh
Susanne Warren
Kathy Webster
Dee Wesbey
Heartha Whitlow
Glenda Wiedermann
Cynthia Wieleba
Emmarie Willcox
Barbara Willey
Joni Williamson
Ann Wilschke
Marge Wilson
Margaret Wilson
Colette Wismer
Patti Wright
Mary Anne Wyse
Jeff Yircott
Sarah Yircott
Kathryn Zerler
Lydia Zick
Marietta Ziebart
Janet Zielke

286

The Krasl Art Center
707 Lake Boulevard
St. Joseph, Michigan 49085
(616) 983-0271

lease send me _____ copies of the **THYME & MONET cookbook** at $16.95 each
lus $3.00 postage and handling per book. Michigan residents please include sales tax.

lame

ddress

ity   State   Zip

Make checks payable to: The Krasl Art Center.

The Krasl Art Center
707 Lake Boulevard
St. Joseph, Michigan 49085
(616) 983-0271

lease send me _____ copies of the **THYME & MONET cookbook** at $16.95 each
lus $3.00 postage and handling per book. Michigan residents please include sales tax.

lame

ddress

ity   State   Zip

Make checks payable to: The Krasl Art Center.